Vocabulary Connections

Rigby • Saxon • Steck-Vaughn

www.HarcourtAchieve.com
1.800.531.5015

ILLUSTRATIONS

Cover: Ed Lindlof
Content Area Logos: Skip Sorvino

Barbara Bash 96–98, 100; Doron Ben-Ami 43–44, 103–105, 107; Nancy Carpenter 55–57, 59, 84–87; Heidi Chang 72–74, 76, 121–122, 124; Eldon Doty 24–26, 28, 108–111, 113; Leslie Evans 7–9, 11, 91–92, 94; Robert Frank 79–81, 83; David Griffin 48–49, 52, 62–63, 65, 72–74, 76, 124; Debbe Heller 32–33, 35, 67–68, 70; Bob Lange 19–20, 22, 50, 115–116, 118; Freya Tanz 12–15, 17, 36–39, 41.

PHOTOGRAPHY

P. 5 © Karen Leeds/The Stock Market; p. 6 © Lee Boltin; p. 18 © William Karel/Sygma; p. 23 © Palm Beach Post, Alan Zlotky/Black Star; p. 29 © Seares/Photo Researchers; pp. 30–31 © John Spragens, Jr./Photo Researchers, Inc.; p. 42 © A.W. Ambler, National Audobon Society/Photo Researchers, Inc.; p. 47 © NASA; p. 53 © Tony Freeman/PhotoEdit; p. 54 © AP/Wide World Photos; p. 66 © AP/Wide World Photos; p. 60 © Bettmann/CORBIS; p. 61 © Duomo/CORBIS; p. 71 © James Schnepf/Gamma-Liaison; p. 77 © David Middleton/Superstock; p. 78 © Stephen Dalton/Photo Researchers, Inc.; p. 90 © Calvin Larsen/Photo Researchers, Inc.; p. 95 © Jerome Wexler/National Audobon Society/ Photo Researchers, Inc.; p. 101 © Shelia Terry, Science Photo Library/Photo Researcers; p. 102 © John Springer Collection/CORBIS; pp. 119 © Hank Morgan/Photo Researchers, Inc.

Additional photography by Photodisc/Getty Royalty Free and Royalty-Free/CORBIS.

ACKNOWLEDGMENTS

HarperCollins Publishers: Adaptation of selection from "The Prophet and the Spider" from *Someone Saw A Spider: Spider Facts and Folktales* by Shirley Climo. Copyright © 1985 by Shirley Climo. Reprinted by permission of HarperCollins Publishers. Adapted and abridged selection from *My Robot Buddy* by Alfred Slote. TEXT COPYRIGHT © 1975 BY ALFRED SLOTE. Used by permission of HarperCollins Publishers.

Houghton Mifflin Company: Excerpt from CARLOTA by Scott O'Dell. Copyright © 1977 by Scott O'Dell. Reprinted by permission of Houghton Mifflin Company. All rights reserved.

Macmillan Publishing Company: Pronunciation Key, reprinted with permission of the publisher from the *Macmillan School Dictionary 2.* Copyright © 1990 Macmillan Publishing Company, a division of Macmillan, Inc.

TABLE OF CONTENTS

CONTENT AREA SYMBOLS . . . . . .

Literature   Social Studies   Science   Mathematics   Health   Fine Arts

BURIED TREASURE

People are fascinated by beautiful and mysterious things. Imagine discovering these treasures buried deep underground. What an experience that would be!

In Lessons 1–4, you will read about different kinds of hidden treasures. You will learn of people who have found buried golden objects or shiny silver under the sea. Get ready to go on a treasure hunt around the world. What treasures would you like to find? Where will you search? Write your ideas on the lines below.

Kinds of Treasures	Places to Search for Treasures
_____	_____
_____	_____
_____	_____
_____	_____

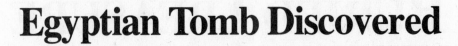

★ Read the selection below. Think about the meanings of the **boldfaced** words. ★

Egyptian Tomb Discovered

Gleaming gold statues, secret treasures, and other objects are all **artifacts**. They tell of a group of people who lived long ago. **Archaeologists** who study such people dreamed of finding these objects in Egypt in the early 1900s. These experts hoped to learn about an ancient **civilization**.

When Egyptian kings died long ago, they were placed in **tombs**. Some tombs were as large as houses. They contained **chambers**, or rooms, where the king and his treasures were buried. Archaeologists searched for these tombs. But all the graves found had been robbed long ago. Only the tomb of King Tutankhamen was still to be found in the area of the **pyramids**, those huge buildings made from stone.

Howard Carter, one archaeologist, was eager to find this tomb. Lord Carnarvon, a rich Englishman, gave Carter the money for the **expedition**. So Carter went to Egypt.

In 1922, Carter's search led him to an ancient entrance. He believed it led to Tutankhamen's tomb. Carter wanted to **investigate** what he had found with Carnarvon. So he sent Carnarvon a letter telling him to come. Together they would closely examine the tomb.

Three weeks later, Carter and Carnarvon were ready to share the **historic** moment when the door to the tomb was opened. It was an important time in history. Carter carefully cut a hole in the door that had been sealed for over three thousand years. Then he held a candle inside the tomb. Carter and Carnarvon saw many riches, including beautiful carved and gold-covered objects. Both were certain that beyond these objects lay King Tutankhamen. It was **evident** that they had found the right tomb.

★ Go back to the story. Underline the words or sentences that give you a clue to the meaning of each **boldfaced** word. ★

CONTEXT CLUES

Read each pair of sentences. Look for a clue in the first sentence to help you choose the missing word in the second sentence. Write the word from the box that completes each sentence.

archaeologists	artifacts	evident	pyramids
chambers	historic	tombs	expedition
investigate	civilization		

1. Some scientists study how people lived long ago. These scientists are called _____.

2. Long ago, a group of people lived in Egypt. That _____ created many beautiful objects.

3. Carter wanted to travel to Egypt to find treasures. He was eager to start his _____.

4. In ancient times, it was difficult to build with massive stones. That is why the _____ amaze us.

5. Egyptian kings were buried in special graves. These _____ were in the desert.

6. A tomb may have several rooms. In one of these _____ the king is buried.

7. Carter couldn't wait to examine the tomb. At last it was time to _____.

8. Discovering the tomb was important. Seeing King Tutankhamen would be an _____ moment.

9. Carter uncovered many precious objects. Some of these _____ were statues and jewels.

10. It was easy to see that Carter was delighted. His joy was _____.

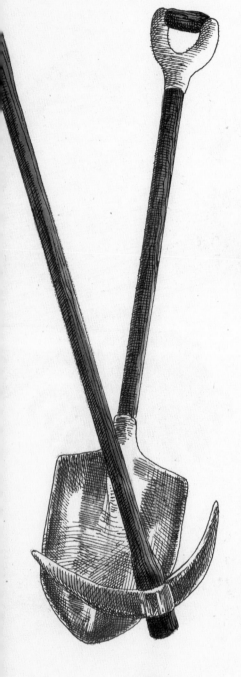

WORD GROUPS

Read each pair of words. Think about how they are alike. Write the word from the box that best completes each group.

expedition	archaeologist	tomb

1. grave, memorial, _____

2. builder, teacher, _____

3. journey, trip, _____

CLOZE PARAGRAPH

Use the words in the box to complete the paragraph. Reread the paragraph to be sure it makes sense.

artifacts	historic	expedition	tomb
archaeologists	investigated	civilization	evident

Less than five months after the opening of King

Tutankhamen's (1) _____, Lord Carnarvon

died. Carter had not yet (2) _____ far enough
into the tomb to find the king, so Carnarvon never saw
Tutankhamen's true resting place. Carnarvon's death caused

him to miss the (3) _____ moment when
Tutankhamen's golden mask was seen for the first time in
thousands of years. The ancient Egyptian

(4) _____ produced not only this beautiful

object, but other remarkable (5) _____ as well.

(6) _____ everywhere were amazed. One

thing was (7) _____. The discoveries from

Carter's (8) _____ would remain one of the
world's greatest treasures.

CROSSWORD PUZZLE

Use the clues and the words in the box to complete the crossword puzzle.

expedition	evident	chambers	tombs
archaeologists	artifacts	historic	investigate
pyramids	civilization		

Across

1. to examine closely
4. scientists who study the people and customs of ancient times
5. huge ancient stone buildings in Egypt
6. places to be buried; graves
7. rooms
8. group of people who live during a certain time and place
9. famous or important in history

Down

2. easy to see or understand
3. a journey for a specific purpose
4. products of human skill

9

GET WISE TO TESTS

Directions: Fill in the space for the word or words that have the same or almost the same meaning as the boldfaced word.

 Be sure to mark the answer space correctly. Do not mark the circle with an X or with a checkmark (✓). Instead, fill in the circle neatly and completely with your pencil.

1. to **investigate** a mystery
   Ⓐ invite
   Ⓑ forget
   Ⓒ write about
   Ⓓ search into

2. the **tombs** of a king
   Ⓕ graves
   Ⓖ bedrooms
   Ⓗ thrones
   Ⓙ palaces

3. a **chamber** in the castle
   Ⓐ floor
   Ⓑ room
   Ⓒ stranger
   Ⓓ ghost

4. a jungle **expedition**
   Ⓕ trip
   Ⓖ animal
   Ⓗ experiment
   Ⓙ tree

5. an **evident** clue
   Ⓐ hidden
   Ⓑ written
   Ⓒ easy to see
   Ⓓ spoken

6. a group of **archaeologists**
   Ⓕ scientists
   Ⓖ bakers
   Ⓗ actors
   Ⓙ tourists

7. an **historic** moment
   Ⓐ important
   Ⓑ common
   Ⓒ funny
   Ⓓ heroic

8. an ancient **civilization**
   Ⓕ disease
   Ⓖ group of people
   Ⓗ tomb
   Ⓙ way of travel

9. build **pyramids**
   Ⓐ huge buildings
   Ⓑ shacks
   Ⓒ houses
   Ⓓ villages

10. **artifacts** discovered
    Ⓕ secrets
    Ⓖ languages
    Ⓗ objects
    Ⓙ people

Writing

Howard Carter and Lord Carnarvon were determined to find the tomb of King Tutankhamen. Have you or someone you know ever worked hard to achieve a difficult goal?

Write a paragraph discussing this goal. What was the goal? Was help needed? Was the goal achieved? Look at the picture for some ideas. Use some vocabulary words in your writing.

_____

_____

_____

_____

_____

_____

_____

_____

_____

_____

_____

_____

_____

Turn to "My Personal Word List" on page 131. Write some words from the story or other words that you would like to know more about. Use a dictionary to find the meanings.

_____

_____

_____

_____

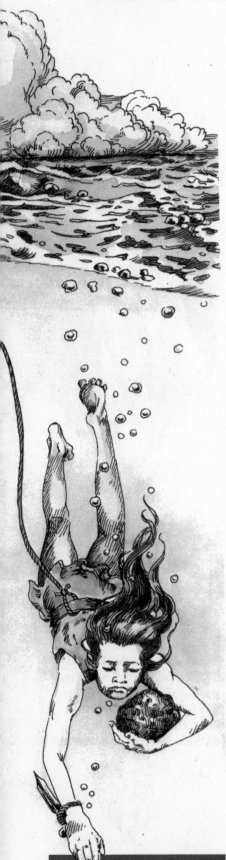

★ Read the selection below. Think about the meanings of the **boldfaced** words. ★

Treasure at Blue Beach

Carlota's family is having a difficult time keeping their ranch going. Carlota and her father have discovered a secret at Blue Beach that may help them survive the troubled times. Carlota tells about their adventure.

"This must have been a large lagoon at one time," my father said when we first discovered the **galleon**. "A good place to hide a ship."

Hidden in the galleon's hold, near the stump of the **mainmast**, were two chests filled with coins. The coins were of pure gold. They showed three castles and the two flying doves that meant they had been struck in the mint at Lima, Peru. The date marked upon each coin that we carried away on the trips we had made was the year of Our Lord 1612.

The two chests — each made of hard wood banded with iron straps and sealed with a hasp that had rusted and fallen off — were well beneath the surface of the water.

There were many things to do before the chests could be reached. Usually it took me half a day to bring up a pouch of coins from the sunken ship.

The place where I dove, which was surrounded by jagged rocks and **driftwood**, was too narrow for my father. He had tried to squeeze through when we first discovered the galleon, but partway down he got stuck and I had to pull him back. It was my task, therefore, to go into the cavelike hole. My father stood beside it and helped me to go down and to come up.

I buckled a strong belt around my waist and to it tied a riata that was ten *varas* long and stout enough to hold a stallion. I fastened my knife to my wrist — a two-edged blade made especially for me by our **blacksmith** — to protect myself against **spiny** rays and the big eels that could sting you to death. In the many dives I had made, I never had seen a shark.

Taking three deep breaths, I prepared to let myself down into the hole. In one hand I held a sink-stone, heavy enough to weigh me down. I let out all the air in my chest, took a deep breath, and held it. Then I began the **descent**.

The sink-stone would have taken me down fast, but the edges of the rocky hole were sharp. I let myself down carefully, one **handhold** at a time. It took me about a minute to reach the rotted deck where the chests lay. I now had two minutes to pry the coins loose and carry them to the surface. We had tried putting the coins in a leather sack and hoisting them to the surface. But we had trouble with this because of the currents that swept around the wreck.

The coins lay in a mass, stuck together, lapping over each other and solid as rock. They looked, when I first saw them, like something left on the stove too long.

The sun was overhead and its rays slanted down through the narrow **crevice**. There were many pieces of **debris** on the deck and I had to step carefully. With my knife I pried loose a handful of coins. They were of a dark green color and speckled here and there with small **barnacles**. I set the coins aside.

My lungs were beginning to hurt, but I had not felt the tug of the riata yet, the signal from my father that I had been down three minutes. I pried loose a second handful and put my knife away. Before the tug came I dropped my sink-stone and took up the coins. Gold is very heavy, much heavier than stones of the same size.

Fish were swimming around me as I went up through the hole of rocks and tree trunks, but I saw no stingrays or eels. I did see a shark lying back on a ledge, but he was small and gray, a sandshark, which is not dangerous.

On my third trip down, I hauled up about the same number of coins as the other times. The pouch we had brought was now full.

From <u>Carlota</u>, by Scott O'Dell

★ Go back to the story. Underline any words or sentences that give you clues to the meanings of the **boldfaced** words. ★

USING CONTEXT

Meanings for the vocabulary words are given below. Go back to the story and read each sentence that has a vocabulary word. If you still cannot tell the meaning, look for clues in the sentences that come before and after the one with the vocabulary word. Write each word in front of its meaning.

driftwood	mainmast	crevice	barnacles
galleon	blacksmith	debris	spiny
handhold	descent		

1. _____: wood that is floating or washed ashore

2. _____: someone who works with metal

3. _____: having sharp points; prickly

4. _____: a downward movement

5. _____: a tall, large ship

6. _____: something to grab for support

7. _____: pole holding a ship's mainsail

8. _____: small, round sea animals that attach themselves to ships

9. _____: scattered remains or pieces of rubbish

10. _____: narrow crack or opening

CHALLENGE YOURSELF

Name two places where you might find a crevice.

_____ _____

Name two objects a blacksmith would make.

_____ _____

COMPOUND WORDS

A **compound word** is made up of two or more words. For example, sail and boat make up the compound word sailboat. Read each meaning on the right. Then write a compound word from the box that goes with the meaning.

handhold	mainmast	blacksmith	driftwood

1. _____: wood that is floating in the water or washed ashore

2. _____: pole that supports the mainsail

3. _____: a hold or grip for the hand

4. _____: a smith or ironworker who makes metal objects by using fire

WORD ORIGINS

A **word origin** is the history of a word. Knowing where a word comes from can help you understand its meaning. Read each word origin. Then write each word from the box in front of its origin.

crevice	debris	barnacles	descent
galleon	spiny		

1. _____ from Latin spina, thorn

2. _____ from Old Spanish galeon, ship

3. _____ from Old French crever, to split

4. _____ from Latin descendere, de- the opposite of, and scend climb

5. _____ from Old French debrisier, to break up in pieces

6. _____ from Middle English bernekke, looking like a goose egg

15

GET WISE TO TESTS

Directions: Read each sentence. Pick the word that best completes the sentence. Mark the answer space for that word.

Some tests put letters before the answer choices. Be sure to find the letter of the answer you think is correct, and then fill in the circle beside it.

1. He was the captain of the _____.
   Ⓐ mainmast Ⓒ serving
   Ⓑ spiny Ⓓ galleon

2. He was caught on the _____ cactus.
   Ⓕ spiny Ⓗ crevice
   Ⓖ debris Ⓙ descent

3. The child fell in the _____.
   Ⓐ spiny Ⓒ crevice
   Ⓑ careless Ⓓ barnacles

4. Scrub the _____ from the ship.
   Ⓕ barnacles Ⓗ aware
   Ⓖ mainmast Ⓙ absorb

5. She grabbed the first _____.
   Ⓐ handhold Ⓒ grant
   Ⓑ spiny Ⓓ gently

6. The wreck left a lot of _____.
   Ⓕ wrapping Ⓗ galleon
   Ⓖ debris Ⓙ actual

7. The sailor climbed up the _____.
   Ⓐ descent Ⓒ awkward
   Ⓑ cautiously Ⓓ mainmast

8. There was _____ on the shore.
   Ⓕ handhold Ⓗ casual
   Ⓖ driftwood Ⓙ painful

9. The climber made a graceful _____ down the mountain.
   Ⓐ crevice Ⓒ dangerous
   Ⓑ below Ⓓ descent

10. The _____ uses fire to melt metal.
    Ⓕ blacksmith Ⓗ driftwood
    Ⓖ dangerous Ⓙ sharply

Review

1. The castle had many _____.
   Ⓐ chambers Ⓒ downstairs
   Ⓑ cold Ⓓ grass

2. Some kings were buried in _____.
   Ⓕ mirrors Ⓗ tombs
   Ⓖ bluebird Ⓙ hollow

3. Their _____ went to Egypt.
   Ⓐ water Ⓒ breezy
   Ⓑ house Ⓓ expedition

4. We studied the old _____.
   Ⓕ ancient Ⓗ hunger
   Ⓖ artifacts Ⓙ create

Carlota's father had said that the lagoon was a good place to hide a ship. Why do you think the ship went into the lagoon? If the crew left the ship, why do you think they left the treasure behind?

Put yourself back in the 1600s. Pretend that you are a crew member of the galleon shown in the picture. Write a journal entry that tells what happened to you and your ship. Use some vocabulary words in your writing.

March 15, 1685

I must write this entry quickly. _____

_____

_____

_____

_____

_____

_____

_____

_____

_____

_____

_____

_____

_____

_____

Turn to "My Personal Word List" on page 131. Write some words from the story or other words that you would like to know more about. Use a dictionary to find the meanings.

★ Read the story below. Think about the meanings of
the **boldfaced** words. ★

Gems

Picture the inside of the earth as a giant cooking pot. Over 100
miles deep inside the earth, it is very hot. The temperature can
reach 2,500° **Fahrenheit**. This heat causes minerals to form.
Some of these minerals become very hard stones that reflect
light.

Over time, these stones are forced upward. They break
through the earth's **mantle**, a layer near the top. It takes time
and hard work to **unearth** the stones. But once they are dug up,
they can be sold.

The stones that are worth a lot of money are called **gems**.
People are willing to pay high prices for two reasons. First,
gems are very rare. They can be found only in certain places
throughout the world. The second reason is that people enjoy
looking at gems. They **glimmer**, shining in the light like
nothing else in nature.

For thousands of years, people have valued gems for their
beauty. Gems have been used in **bracelets**, which are worn on
the arm. They are also used in rings and other kinds of **jewelry**.
The most high-priced gem is the diamond. It is more special
than other gems because of its hardness and clear brightness.

Emeralds, which are green, are almost as valuable as
diamonds. A large, perfectly shaped emerald can be worth
more than a smaller diamond. The **ruby**, the red gem, is next in
value. It is not as hard as an emerald or a diamond. But some
people think rubies are more beautiful than any other gem. The
sapphire is a blue gem. It is also rich in color, but is not as rare
as a ruby.

People think of gems as works of art created by nature. For
that reason, precious gems can be found in museums around
the world.

★ Go back to the story. Underline the words or sentences that give
you a clue to the meaning of each **boldfaced** word. ★

CONTEXT CLUES

Read each sentence. Look for clues to help you complete each
sentence with a word from the box. Write the word on the line.

bracelets	jewelry	Gems	Emeralds
Fahrenheit	unearth	ruby	glimmer
mantle	sapphire		

1. _____, or precious stones, are expensive
   because they are so rare.

2. One reason gems are attractive is that they
   _____ when light hits them.

3. Gems form inside the earth where temperatures reach
   2,500 degrees _____.

4. Miners find gems above the earth's _____,
   a layer near the top of the earth.

5. When workers _____ them, the gems do
   not look as attractive as polished stones.

6. Gems are used for many things. Their most common use is
   in rings and other _____.

7. _____, which are green, are the birthstone
   for May.

8. The red _____ is the birthstone for July.

9. The _____, which is usually blue, is the
   birthstone for September.

10. Precious stones may be used in necklaces worn on the neck,
    or in _____ worn on the arm.

CHALLENGE YOURSELF

Name two things that <u>glimmer</u>.

_____   _____

ANALOGIES

An **analogy** shows how two words go together in the same way as two other words. For example, <u>robin</u> is to <u>bird</u> as <u>daisy</u> is to <u>flower</u>. Write the words from the box to complete the following analogies.

ruby	bracelet	sapphire	jewelry

1. <u>Snow</u> is to <u>white</u> as _____ is to <u>blue</u>.

2. <u>Ring</u> is to <u>finger</u> as _____ is to <u>wrist</u>.

3. <u>Apple</u> is to <u>fruit</u> as <u>necklace</u> is to _____.

4. <u>Grass</u> is to <u>emerald</u> as <u>apple</u> is to _____.

DICTIONARY SKILLS

Guide words are the two words at the top of each dictionary page. They show the first and last entries on that page. All the word entries in between are in alphabetical order. Look at the pairs of guide words. On the lines below each pair, write the words from the box that would appear on the same dictionary page. Be sure to put them in alphabetical order.

Fahrenheit	mantle	emerald	gems
glimmer	unearth	jewelry	sapphire

earn / hit

_____

_____

_____

jazz / uneven

_____

_____

_____

Directions: Read the phrase. Look for the word or words that have the same or almost the same meaning as the boldfaced word. Mark the answer space for your choice.

 Tip Some tests have letters in the answer space. Be sure to find the letter of the answer you think is correct. Then fill in that circle.

1. golden **bracelets**
   Ⓐ gifts
   Ⓑ lost treasures
   Ⓒ arm jewelry
   Ⓓ keys

2. degrees in **Fahrenheit**
   Ⓕ measure of temperature
   Ⓖ type of water
   Ⓗ hot water
   Ⓙ first-aid method

3. **unearth** the treasure
   Ⓐ steal
   Ⓑ hide
   Ⓒ uncover
   Ⓓ paint

4. perfect **emeralds**
   Ⓕ green gems
   Ⓖ red gems
   Ⓗ blue gems
   Ⓙ yellow gems

5. **mantle** of earth
   Ⓐ size
   Ⓑ model
   Ⓒ layer
   Ⓓ piece

6. **glimmer** of light
   Ⓕ glow
   Ⓖ hill
   Ⓗ candle
   Ⓙ idea

7. rare **ruby**
   Ⓐ yellow gem
   Ⓑ blue gem
   Ⓒ red gem
   Ⓓ green gem

8. fancy **jewelry**
   Ⓕ shirts and hats
   Ⓖ gloves and stockings
   Ⓗ rings and pins
   Ⓙ purses and wallets

9. beautiful **gems**
   Ⓐ colorful pebbles
   Ⓑ precious stones
   Ⓒ space rocks
   Ⓓ huge rocks

10. expensive **sapphire**
    Ⓕ green gem
    Ⓖ red gem
    Ⓗ blue gem
    Ⓙ yellow gem

Review

1. jungle **expedition**
   Ⓐ costume
   Ⓑ custom
   Ⓒ exhibit
   Ⓓ trip

2. ancient **civilization**
   Ⓕ large statues
   Ⓖ lost treasures
   Ⓗ group of people
   Ⓙ vacation

3. careful **descent**
   Ⓐ moving down
   Ⓑ choice
   Ⓒ design
   Ⓓ moving up

4. unwanted **debris**
   Ⓕ treasures
   Ⓖ remains
   Ⓗ leaders
   Ⓙ books

5. deep **crevice**
   Ⓐ water
   Ⓑ canyon
   Ⓒ valley
   Ⓓ opening

Imagine that you have been given a basket full of rare gems. What objects would you make with them? You might make some jewelry, a statue, or some useful objects.

On the lines below, describe the objects you would make. Also tell what you might do with the objects. Use some vocabulary words in your writing.

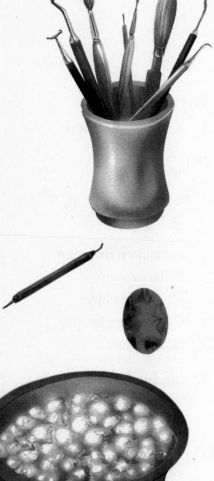

Turn to "My Personal Word List" on page 131. Write some words from the story or other words that you would like to know more about. Use a dictionary to find the meanings.

_____
_____
_____
_____
_____
_____
_____
_____
_____
_____
_____
_____
_____
_____
_____
_____
_____

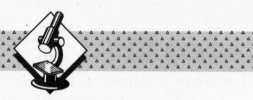

★ Read the story below. Think about the meanings of the **boldfaced** words. ★

Treasures From the Deep

On a sunny September morning in 1622, a fleet of 28 ships set sail from Cuba. Their **destination** was Spain. The ships had come to America to gather riches for King Philip. Now they were headed home with treasure. Before two days had passed, however, the ships were hit by a howling hurricane. The ships were sunk off the coast of Florida. The crew and the treasure were lost beneath the waves.

Over the years many treasure hunters searched for the **sunken** *Atocha*. Yet it was not until 1972 that the *Atocha* was found. The **discoverers** were Mel Fisher and Bob Holloway. They had worked for more than five years to find the ship.

It is not an easy task to search for **undersea** treasure. Through the years, the ocean had wrecked the ship and buried the **hull**. The ship's body was under shifting sands. Fisher and Holloway used two boats in their search. They had to **navigate**, or steer, their boats through rough waters. At times the swelling waves hit the ships. These **billows** filled them with water.

The two search boats carried different equipment. Holloway's boat carried magnets that could find metal far below the surface. When magnets showed **evidence** of metal, Holloway threw a **buoy** into the water. This was a signal to Fisher. Now Fisher knew where he and his team should go to work. The second boat carried digging tools and diving gear. Fisher told his **scuba** divers to get ready. They put on wet suits and air tanks and slipped into the water.

The first dives were disappointing. But, then one day, a diver burst to the surface. In his hand were gold necklaces! This was only the beginning. Divers found gold coins and bars of silver. They found cups decorated with emeralds. The *Atocha* had released its treasure from the deep at last!

★ Go back to the story. Underline the words or sentences that give you a clue to the meaning of each **boldfaced** word. ★

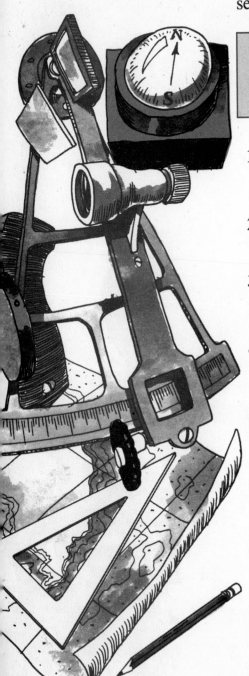

CONTEXT CLUES

Read each pair of sentences. Look for a clue in the first sentence to help you choose the missing word in the second sentence. Write the word from the box that completes each sentence.

discoverers	sunken	undersea	hull
destination	billows	buoy	scuba
navigate	evidence		

1. In 1622, the *Atocha* sank beneath the sea. The

    _____ ship remained hidden for 350 years.

2. The ship had set out for Spain. This _____
    was its home country.

3. The sailors knew how to handle the ship. But they could

    not _____ it through a hurricane.

4. The sails and rigging of the *Atocha* were torn away. Only

    the _____ was left, and it soon sank.

5. Centuries later, people found clues to the location of the

    lost ship. Now there was real _____.

6. The men who found the *Atocha* worked secretly. These

    _____ wanted to protect their find.

7. A weighted floating object was used as a signal. The

    _____ marked a possible treasure site.

8. Working underwater requires careful planning.

    An _____ job is not easy.

9. Divers worked from small boats despite the huge waves.

    These _____ nearly overturned the boats.

10. The divers used special breathing gear. The

    _____ equipment made their work easier.

WORD ORIGINS

Remember that a **word origin** is the history of a word. Knowing where a word comes from can help you understand its meaning. Read each word origin. Then write each word from the box in front of its origin.

| evidence | hull | navigate | scuba |

1. _____ from Latin n<u>avis</u>, ship, and <u>iglare</u>, to drive

2. _____ from Dutch <u>hol</u>, hold

3. _____ from Latin <u>videre</u>, to see

4. _____ first letters of its description — self-contained underwater breathing apparatus

CLOZE PARAGRAPH

Use the words in the box to complete the paragraph. Reread the paragraph to be sure it makes sense.

| discoverers | sunken | billows | buoy |
| destination | undersea | | |

Lots of treasure may be hidden (1) _____.

But in the search for a (2) _____ ship, divers have to worry about such threats as sharks. Divers also have to

be concerned about strong winds and (3) _____

of waves. A (4) _____ is often used as a marker

so that divers can find their (5) _____, the place

where the treasure lies. If divers become (6) _____ of treasure, their hard work will have been rewarded.

WORD MAP

Use the vocabulary words in the box to complete the word map about buried treasure. Add other words that you know to each group. One heading will not have any vocabulary words, but only your words.

| sunken | discoverers | scuba | undersea | buoy |

Who Finds Treasure

1. _____
2. _____
3. _____
4. _____
5. _____

Where Treasure Is Found

1. _____
2. _____
3. _____
4. _____
5. _____

BURIED TREASURE

Things Used to Hunt Treasure

1. _____
2. _____
3. _____
4. _____
5. _____

Kinds of Treasure Found

1. _____
2. _____
3. _____
4. _____
5. _____

Directions: Read the sentences. Look for the best word to use in the blank. Mark the answer space for your choice.

 Tip If you are not sure which word completes the sentence, do the best you can. Try to choose the answer that makes the most sense.

1. The treasure lay at the bottom of the ocean. It was in a _____ ship.
   - Ⓐ foreign
   - Ⓒ scuba
   - Ⓑ sunken
   - Ⓓ new

2. The search team set out. Their _____ was the Florida coast.
   - Ⓕ destination
   - Ⓗ discoverer
   - Ⓖ evidence
   - Ⓙ buoy

3. They used underwater equipment. This _____ gear allowed them to breathe.
   - Ⓐ space
   - Ⓒ scuba
   - Ⓑ camping
   - Ⓓ sunken

4. Parts of the ship had been destroyed. The _____ lay on the ocean floor.
   - Ⓕ billows
   - Ⓗ fish
   - Ⓖ watch
   - Ⓙ hull

5. The crew had tried to save the ship. They could not _____ through a storm.
   - Ⓐ argue
   - Ⓒ agree
   - Ⓑ navigate
   - Ⓓ discover

6. The weather sank the ship. It was turned over by wind and strong _____.
   - Ⓕ evidence
   - Ⓗ rafts
   - Ⓖ billows
   - Ⓙ driftwood

7. The divers got ready. They were prepared for their _____ mission.
   - Ⓐ glimmering
   - Ⓒ undersea
   - Ⓑ high
   - Ⓓ careless

8. They looked for proof of the ship. They found the _____ they wanted.
   - Ⓕ evidence
   - Ⓗ magic
   - Ⓖ billows
   - Ⓙ discoverers

9. They used a marker to locate the ship. This _____ floated on top of the water.
   - Ⓐ destination
   - Ⓒ billow
   - Ⓑ swimmer
   - Ⓓ buoy

10. They found the treasure. As the _____, they were allowed to keep it.
    - Ⓕ driftwood
    - Ⓗ billows
    - Ⓖ discoverers
    - Ⓙ losers

Review

1. A diamond is very valuable. A red _____ is valuable, too.
   - Ⓐ ruby
   - Ⓒ glass
   - Ⓑ mantle
   - Ⓓ emerald

2. She wore many rings. Her _____ shone in the light.
   - Ⓕ moon
   - Ⓗ tires
   - Ⓖ jewelry
   - Ⓙ center

Writing

Suppose you have just read about the discovery of a sunken ship. You want to join the search team that will try to find lost treasures.

Write a letter to the person in charge of the search. Convince him or her that you should be chosen for the team. Use some vocabulary words in your writing.

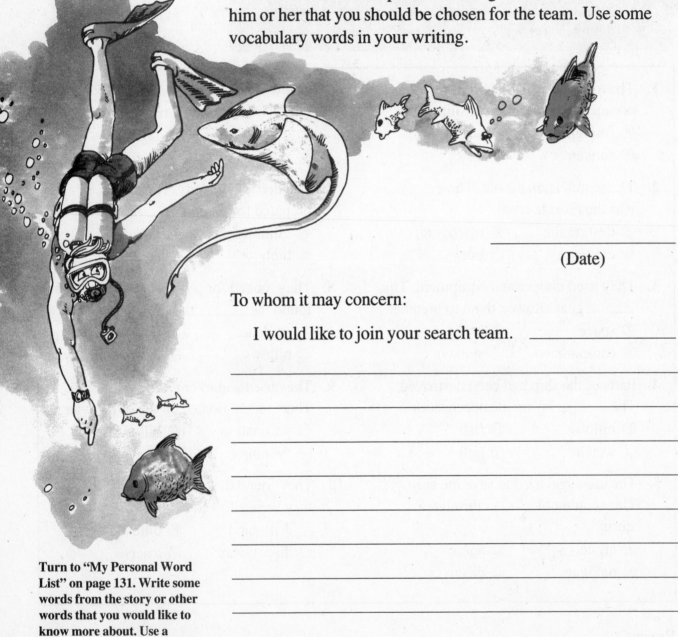

_____
(Date)

To whom it may concern:

I would like to join your search team. _____

_____

_____

_____

_____

_____

_____

_____

_____

Sincerely,

_____
(your name)

Turn to "My Personal Word List" on page 131. Write some words from the story or other words that you would like to know more about. Use a dictionary to find the meanings.

★ To review the words in Lessons 1–4, turn to page 125. ★

UP, UP, AND AWAY

Flights can be long or short, safe or dangerous. They can be in spaceships, hot-air balloons, and airplanes. They can be for science, business, or just for fun.

In Lessons 5–8, you will read about things that fly. Imagine flying high in the sky in a hot-air balloon. Think about words that describe how you feel as you fly up, up, and away. What do you see fly by your balloon? Birds? Airplanes? Think about things that fly. Write your ideas under the headings below.

Feelings About Flying   **Things That Fly**

_____   _____

_____   _____

_____   _____

_____   _____

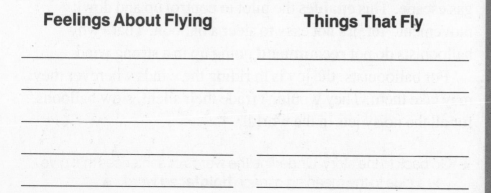

★ Read the story below. Think about the meanings of the **boldfaced** words. ★

Ballooning

Huge, round, and colorful, they float together through the clear sky. They flash in the sun and look like **fabulous** beads from a giant's necklace. But they are really balloons. Their passengers are out for a day of fun. In the United States alone, more than 5,000 people **devote** their free time to ballooning. They spend as many hours as they can up in the air.

Ballooning began in France in 1783. There, the Montgolfier brothers built the first balloon. It was 35 feet in diameter. They filled it with hot air and it **expanded**. Then they let the ropes go and sent it **aloft**. It was a great success. They built a second balloon and added three passengers — a duck, a rooster, and a sheep. It was a great surprise to everyone. The hot air in the balloon began to escape. Eight minutes later the animals landed safely.

In November of 1783 the first manned balloon trip took place. The balloon and its two passengers rose to an **altitude** of 300 feet. For 25 minutes, the balloon floated over the rooftops of Paris. Thousands of people below cheered. They were watching a truly wonderful **feat**. This early successful flight marked the beginning of **aviation**.

Why do balloons rise and float in the air? When a balloon is filled with heated air or a light gas, the bag will rise and become **airborne**. This happens because hot air or gas is lighter than the air outside the bag. The pilot can slowly let the hot air or gas escape. This **enables** the pilot to control up and down movement. Yet, it's not easy to steer a balloon. That's why balloonists do not **recommend** going up in a strong wind.

For balloonists, the joy is in riding the winds wherever they may take them. They wouldn't trade their silent, slow balloons for all the noisy jets in the world!

★ Go back to the story. Underline the words or sentences that give you a clue to the meaning of each **boldfaced** word. ★

CONTEXT CLUES

Read each sentence below. Choose a word from the box that means the same as the underlined part of each sentence. Write the word on the line after the sentence.

fabulous	devote	aloft	altitude	feat
aviation	airborne	enables	recommend	expanded

1. The Montgolfier brothers decided to <u>commit</u> themselves to ballooning. _____

2. The brothers might not <u>advise or suggest</u> ballooning for everyone. _____

3. The Montgolfiers' tests were the first successful form of <u>flying</u>. _____

4. The thought of a person sailing through the air was <u>terrific</u>. _____

5. The Montgolfier brothers knew that the <u>great deed</u> was possible. _____

6. On June 4, 1783, a crowd watched as a big balloon <u>grew larger</u> when gas was pumped into it. _____

7. Gas, which is lighter than air, <u>makes it possible for</u> the balloon to rise. _____

8. As the crowd watched, the balloon sailed upward to a greater <u>height</u>. _____

9. Many were afraid to go <u>up in the air</u> themselves. _____

10. The sight of a balloon that was <u>being carried through the air</u> made the crowd cheer. _____

WRITING SENTENCES

Use each vocabulary word in the box to write an original sentence.

fabulous	airborne	aloft	altitude
feat	expanded		

1. _____

2. _____

3. _____

4. _____

5. _____

6. _____

CLOZE PARAGRAPH

Use the words in the box to complete the paragraph. Reread the paragraph to be sure it makes sense.

recommend	aviation	devote	enables

Many people choose a form of (1) _____ as a sport. In order to pilot a gas or hot-air balloon, a person must follow some rules. He or she must be at least sixteen years old

and (2) _____ at least ten hours to flying lessons. He or she must also pass a written test and be licensed.

Some people (3) _____ entering balloon races. Others just like to drift along peacefully. Ballooning

(4) _____ people to view the world in a most unusual way.

TANGLED-UP WORDS

A word is underlined in each sentence below. The word sounds similar to a word in the box. But its meaning makes it the wrong word for the sentence.

Read the paragraphs. Find the word in the box that should replace the underlined word. Write the vocabulary word on the line next to the number of the underlined word.

fabulous	devote	expanded	altitude
aviation	airborne	enables	recommended
feat	aloft		

I always told my friends, "You'll never find me flying in the sky because (1) addition is not for me!" Then one day my cousin proudly (2) pretended a hang glider. A hang glider is like a large kite. It (3) labels a person to glide through the air at a high (4) attitude.

"It sounds like an impossible (5) feet," I said. Still, I tried it. I perched myself at the top of a cliff. Then I jumped. I (6) excited my wings and held my breath. The valley spread out below. I was flying like a bird (7) aloud. It felt (8) famous. Now I am (9) newborn at least once a week. If I could, I'd (10) devour all my time to hang gliding!

1. _____   6. _____

2. _____   7. _____

3. _____   8. _____

4. _____   9. _____

5. _____   10. _____

GET WISE TO TESTS

Directions: Fill in the space for the word or words that have the same or almost the same meaning as the boldfaced word.

 Think about the meaning of the **boldfaced** word. Don't be fooled by a word that looks similar to it.

Review

1. lucky **discoverers**
   - Ⓐ traders
   - Ⓑ finders
   - Ⓒ winners
   - Ⓓ designers

2. **navigate** the boat
   - Ⓕ steer
   - Ⓖ fix
   - Ⓗ sell
   - Ⓙ lose

3. hidden **chambers**
   - Ⓐ treasures
   - Ⓑ letters
   - Ⓒ rooms
   - Ⓓ messages

4. ship's **hull**
   - Ⓕ main part
   - Ⓖ head of crew
   - Ⓗ sailors
   - Ⓙ problem

5. **evident** answer
   - Ⓐ hidden
   - Ⓑ wrong
   - Ⓒ clear
   - Ⓓ strange

1. **recommend** action
   - Ⓐ stop
   - Ⓑ recall
   - Ⓒ suggest
   - Ⓓ complete

2. **fabulous** story
   - Ⓕ lengthy
   - Ⓖ famous
   - Ⓗ believable
   - Ⓙ terrific

3. size **expanded**
   - Ⓐ grew
   - Ⓑ released
   - Ⓒ exploded
   - Ⓓ matched

4. gaining **altitude**
   - Ⓕ attention
   - Ⓖ height
   - Ⓗ wealth
   - Ⓙ weight

5. **airborne** jet
   - Ⓐ flying
   - Ⓑ rolling
   - Ⓒ overlooking
   - Ⓓ broken

6. **enables** flight
   - Ⓕ forbids
   - Ⓖ teaches
   - Ⓗ admires
   - Ⓙ allows

7. **aviation** classes
   - Ⓐ average
   - Ⓑ swimming
   - Ⓒ flying
   - Ⓓ dancing

8. **devote** time
   - Ⓕ devour
   - Ⓖ commit
   - Ⓗ find
   - Ⓙ refuse

9. amazing **feat**
   - Ⓐ deed
   - Ⓑ fellow
   - Ⓒ time
   - Ⓓ area

10 bird **aloft**
   - Ⓕ upside-down
   - Ⓖ in the air
   - Ⓗ in the yard
   - Ⓙ sideways

Imagine that you have just completed two short flights, one in a hot-air balloon and one in an airplane. How were the flights alike? How were they different?

On the lines below, compare and contrast your flights. The picture below may help with ideas. Use some vocabulary words in your writing.

Flight is a wonderful experience in either a hot-air balloon

or an airplane. Both of them _____

_____

_____

_____

_____

_____

Turn to "My Personal Word List" on page 131. Write some words from the story or other words that you would like to know more about. Use a dictionary to find the meanings.

_____

_____

_____

_____

_____

_____

_____

★ Read the story below. Think about the meanings of the **boldfaced** words. ★

Icarus and Daedalus

In this ancient Greek legend, Daedalus and his son, Icarus, plan an escape from the island of Crete. What happens when Icarus does not listen to his father's warning about their daring flight?

Among all those **mortals** who grew so wise that they learned the secrets of the gods, none was more cunning than Daedalus.

He once built, for King Minos of Crete, a wonderful Labyrinth of winding ways so cunningly tangled up and twisted around that, once inside, you could never find your way out again without a magic clue. But the king's favor **veered** with the wind, and one day he had his master architect **imprisoned** in a tower. Daedalus managed to escape from his cell; but it seemed impossible to leave the island, since every ship that came or went was well guarded by order of the king.

At length, watching the sea-gulls in the air — the only creatures that were sure of liberty — he thought of a plan for himself and his young son Icarus, who was **captive** with him.

Little by little, he gathered a store of feathers great and small. He fastened these together with thread, molded them in with wax, and so fashioned two great wings like those of a bird. When they were done, Daedalus fitted them to his own shoulders, and after one or two efforts, he found that by waving his arms he could winnow the air and cleave it, as a swimmer does the sea. He held himself aloft, wavered this way and that with the wind, and at last, like a great fledgling, he learned to fly.

Without delay, he fell to work on a pair of wings for the boy Icarus, and taught him carefully how to use them, bidding him beware of rash adventures among the stars. "Remember," said the father, "never to fly very low or very high, for the fogs about the earth would weigh you down, but the blaze of the sun will surely melt your feathers apart if you go too near."

For Icarus, these cautions went in at one ear and out by the other. Who could remember to be careful when he was to fly for the first time? Are birds careful? Not they! And not an idea remained in the boy's head but the one joy of escape.

The day came, and the fair wind that was to set them free. The father bird put on his wings, and, while the light urged them to be gone, he waited to see that all was well with Icarus, for the two could not fly hand in hand. Up they rose, the boy after his father.

At first there was a terror in the joy. The wide vacancy of the air dazed them — a glance downward made their brains **reel**. But when a great wind filled their wings, and Icarus felt himself **sustained**, like a halcyonbird in the hollow of a wave, like a child **uplifted** by his mother, he forgot everything in the world but joy. He forgot Crete and the other islands that he had passed over: he saw but **vaguely** that winged thing in the distance before him that was his father Daedalus. He longed for one **draft** of flight to quench the thirst of his captivity: he stretched out his arms to the sky and made towards the highest heavens.

Alas for him! Warmer and warmer grew the air. Those arms, that had seemed to uphold him, relaxed. His wings wavered, drooped. He fluttered his young hands vainly — he was falling — and in that terror he remembered. The heat of the sun had melted the wax from his wings; the feathers were falling, one by one, like snowflakes; and there was none to help.

He fell like a leaf tossed down the wind, down, down, with one cry that **overtook** Daedalus far away. When he returned, and sought high and low for the poor boy, he saw nothing but the bird-like feathers afloat on the water, and he knew that Icarus was drowned.

The nearest island he named Icaria, in memory of the child; but he, in heavy grief, went to the temple of Apollo in Sicily, and there hung up his wings as an offering. Never again did he attempt to fly.

From Old Greek Folk Stories Told Anew, by Josephine Preston

★ Go back to the story. Underline any words or sentences that give you clues to the meanings of the **boldfaced** words. ★

USING CONTEXT

Meanings for the vocabulary words are given below. Go back to the story and read each sentence that has a vocabulary word. If you still cannot tell the meaning, look for clues in the sentences that come before and after the one with the vocabulary word. Write each word in front of its meaning.

captive	draft	mortals	reel
overtook	imprisoned	vaguely	veered
sustained	uplifted		

1. _____ : beings who must die; humans who do not have the power of gods

2. _____ : to spin; become dizzy

3. _____ : animal or person taken and held without permission

4. _____ : caught up with

5. _____ : a drink

6. _____ : not clearly

7. _____ : raised

8. _____ : changed or shifted direction

9. _____ : locked up; put into a jail

10. _____ : held up or supported

CHALLENGE YOURSELF

Name two kinds of mortals.

_____   _____

Name two places to imprison someone.

_____   _____

SYNONYMS

Synonyms are words that have the same or almost the same meaning. Read each underlined word on the left. Circle its synonym on the right

1. captive   captain   prisoner   happy

2. sustained   supported   released   flew

3. draft   trail   persuade   drink

4. reel   actual   whirl   shock

5. veer   shift   address   escape

6. uplifted   dropped   raised   grown

ANTONYMS

Antonyms are words that have opposite meanings. Write a word from the box that is an antonym for the underlined word in each sentence.

imprisoned	vaguely	overtook
uplifted	mortals	captive

1. Could you see it <u>clearly</u> or _____?

2. The winner _____ the other runner, who <u>retreated</u>.

3. One button <u>lowered</u> the plane, and the other

   button _____ it.

4. For ten years they were _____, and then they were <u>freed</u>.

5. While the <u>gods</u> live forever, _____ on earth do not.

6. Was he _____, or was he <u>free</u>?

39

GET WISE TO TESTS

Directions: Read each sentence. Pick the word that best completes the sentence. Mark the answer space for that word.

 Some tests put letters before the answer choices. Be sure to find the letter of the answer you think is correct, and then fill in the circle beside it.

1. The wild animal was _____ in a cage.
   Ⓐ reeled   Ⓒ vaguely
   Ⓑ mortal   Ⓓ imprisoned

2. _____ don't have the powers of the gods.
   Ⓕ Mortals   Ⓗ Veered
   Ⓖ Drafts   Ⓙ Helpless

3. We _____ our bikes to avoid hitting a tree.
   Ⓐ captive   Ⓒ overtook
   Ⓑ veered   Ⓓ current

4. The prisoner was held _____ in the jail.
   Ⓕ mortals   Ⓗ vaguely
   Ⓖ softly   Ⓙ captive

5. The bird was _____ in the air by its wings.
   Ⓐ sustained   Ⓒ draft
   Ⓑ sunk   Ⓓ vaguely

6. A _____ of water was all the thirsty hiker wanted.
   Ⓕ captive   Ⓗ draft
   Ⓖ reel   Ⓙ sustained

7. The baby was _____ and put into her father's arms.
   Ⓐ mortals   Ⓒ uplifted
   Ⓑ draft   Ⓓ reel

8. I _____ remember seeing that show long ago.
   Ⓕ draft   Ⓗ peacefully
   Ⓖ regret   Ⓙ vaguely

9. The fast ride made our heads _____.
   Ⓐ daze   Ⓒ mortals
   Ⓑ reel   Ⓓ captive

10. The speeding car soon _____ the slow truck.
    Ⓕ overtook   Ⓗ uplifted
    Ⓖ frequent   Ⓙ draft

Review

1. I could not breathe due to the high _____.
   Ⓐ prices   Ⓒ altitude
   Ⓑ happy   Ⓓ sail

2. She will _____ many hours to practicing the piano.
   Ⓕ lose   Ⓗ apples
   Ⓖ devote   Ⓙ awake

Pretend that you have been asked to write a science fiction story for a magazine telling about your ability to fly.

On the lines below, describe your flight. How did it feel? Where did you go? What did you do? Use some vocabulary words in your writing.

_____

_____

_____

_____

_____

_____

_____

_____

_____

_____

_____

_____

_____

_____

_____

_____

_____

_____

_____

Turn to "My Personal Word List" on page 131. Write some words from the story or other words that you would like to know more about. Use a dictionary to find the meanings.

★ Read the story below. Think about the meanings of the **boldfaced** words. ★

Night Flights

Night falls softly over the hill. The air clicks and hums with insects. Suddenly thousands of little bats fly out of a cave. They rise up in great circles and head off into the night. Clouds of bats continue coming from the cave for about an hour. Before the night is over, each one will eat 10,000 insects.

Many people have mistaken ideas about bats. Of all the 900 **species** of bats, not one kind is the **fearsome** creature seen in scary movies. Bats **prey** on insects, not people. They are timid like their **rodent** cousins, mice. It is not true, either, that bats are blind. Although many kinds have weak **eyesight** at night, a few kinds can see quite well.

Bats look quite different from one another. The largest are called fox bats. These bats are five feet across when their wings are spread. But the bumblebee bat weighs less than an ounce. It is the world's smallest mammal.

Most bats use echoes to help them fly. As a bat flies, it sends out short, high sounds. These sounds bounce back and tell the bat what lies ahead. Maybe it's an **obstacle** to fly around, like a tree or a person! Another kind of echo might tell that an insect is near. Echoes help bats **distinguish** among the many different things around them.

The female bat carries her newborn pup with her as she hunts for food. When it is six to eight weeks old, this young bat is ready for test flights on its own. For some species, the longest flight will be when it comes time for **migration**. At that time, bats fly to a warm place for the winter season. Some bats fly over 800 miles! Many kinds of bats **hibernate** during cold weather. They find quiet, safe places to sleep. When spring returns, they will leave their **habitat**, the cave. Once again they will be on the hunt for insects in the dead of night.

★ Go back to the story. Underline the words or sentences that give you a clue to the meaning of each **boldfaced** word. ★

USING CONTEXT

Meanings for the vocabulary words are given below. Go back to the story and read each sentence that has a vocabulary word. If you still cannot tell the meaning, look for clues in the sentences that come before and after the one with the vocabulary word. Write each word in front of its meaning.

prey	habitat	obstacle	distinguish
fearsome	eyesight	hibernate	rodent
species	migration		

1. _____ : a mammal that gnaws with its teeth, such as a mouse, bat, or squirrel

2. _____ : tell the difference between

3. _____ : group of animals or plants that are alike in many ways

4. _____ : frightening

5. _____ : to hunt animals for food

6. _____ : vision

7. _____ : to spend the winter asleep

8. _____ : something that gets in the way

9. _____ : movement from one place to another when seasons change

10. _____ : the place where a plant or animal usually lives

CHALLENGE YOURSELF

Name two animals whose <u>habitat</u> is a tree.

_____

Name two <u>fearsome</u> creatures.

_____

DICTIONARY SKILLS

Turn to page 133 in the Dictionary. Use the **pronunciation key** to help you learn how to say the vocabulary words in ( ) in the sentences below. Write the regular spelling for each word in ( ).

1. During (mī grā′shən) bats fly to a warm place. _____

2. There are many (spē′shēz) of bats. _____

3. Most bats have poor (ī ′sīt′). _____

4. Bats (hī′ bər nāt′) in the winter. _____

5. Can you (di sting′gwish) between a bat and a crow? _____

6. Bats (prā) on insects. _____

7. A pond is a (hab′ i tat′) for forms of life. _____

8. Many people think bats look (fîr′səm). _____

CLASSIFYING

Read the words in each list and decide how they are alike. Above each list, write a word from the box that fits both words.

obstacles	rodents	fearsome	habitats
prey	species		

1. _____
   roadblock
   fallen tree

2. _____
   mouse
   bat

3. _____
   lions
   tigers

4. _____
   angry bear
   scary mask

5. _____
   nest
   cave

6. _____
   insects
   small animals

Directions: Read each sentence carefully. Then choose the best answer to complete each sentence. Mark the space for the answer you have chosen.

Tip

Before you choose your answer, try reading the sentence with each answer choice. This will help you choose an answer that makes sense.

1. If you belong to a **species**, you belong to a _____.
   - Ⓐ factory
   - Ⓒ group
   - Ⓑ church
   - Ⓓ rodent

2. When an animal is **fearsome**, it is _____.
   - Ⓕ pleasant
   - Ⓗ old
   - Ⓖ frightening
   - Ⓙ scarce

3. An animal that will **prey** is one that will _____.
   - Ⓐ hunt
   - Ⓒ forget
   - Ⓑ hibernate
   - Ⓓ dive

4. A **rodent** is a kind of _____.
   - Ⓕ animal
   - Ⓗ migration
   - Ⓖ companion
   - Ⓙ shape

5. Your **eyesight** allows you to _____.
   - Ⓐ sing
   - Ⓒ see
   - Ⓑ whisper
   - Ⓓ disagree

6. A **habitat** is a place where something or someone _____.
   - Ⓕ preys
   - Ⓗ directs
   - Ⓖ travels
   - Ⓙ lives

7. An **obstacle** may make a person accidentally _____.
   - Ⓐ finish
   - Ⓒ arrive
   - Ⓑ trip
   - Ⓓ win

8. When you **distinguish** between two things, you can tell a _____.
   - Ⓕ difference
   - Ⓗ habitat
   - Ⓖ secret
   - Ⓙ story

9. **Migration** is a kind of _____.
   - Ⓐ vesting
   - Ⓒ distinguishing
   - Ⓑ reciting
   - Ⓓ traveling

10. When a bear begins to **hibernate**, it _____.
    - Ⓕ sleeps
    - Ⓗ migrates
    - Ⓖ preys
    - Ⓙ roars

Review

1. **Mortals** are _____ beings.
   - Ⓐ living
   - Ⓒ healthy
   - Ⓑ insect
   - Ⓓ foreign

2. Some **captives** are in _____.
   - Ⓕ water
   - Ⓗ traffic
   - Ⓖ prison
   - Ⓙ paint

Bats are animals that are often misunderstood. People are often misunderstood, too. Think of a time when you were misunderstood.

    Write a paragraph describing the experience. What caused the misunderstanding? How did you feel? What did you do? Use some vocabulary words in your writing.

_____

_____

_____

_____

_____

_____

_____

_____

_____

_____

_____

_____

_____

Turn to "My Personal Word List" on page 131. Write some words from the story or other words that you would like to know more about. Use a dictionary to find the meanings.

_____

_____

_____

_____

_____

★ Read the story below. Think about the meanings of
  the **boldfaced** words. ★

Walking in Space

In February 1995, six **dedicated** astronauts sat aboard the
space shuttle *Discovery*. They would live there for the next
eight days. "Four, three, two, one, **liftoff**!" The space shuttle
rose into space.

Dr. Bernard Harris, Jr., was among the six loyal men
crowded into the shuttle's **capsule**. He knew that the flight
would put his name in the history books. He would be the first
African American to walk in space.

Astronauts go through many months of training. They
learn to follow their leader's directions. They also learn to act
quickly when their **commander** gives an order. Each person's
assignment changes from time to time. Learning to do
different kinds of work means that each person can do the work
of another crew member if needed. All crew members are
taught how to use the controls in the **cockpit**. They are also
instructed in other ways of working in that part of the capsule.

The hardest part of the training is getting used to being
weightless. On Earth, the **gravitational** pull of the earth gives
us weight. In space, the pull of the earth on our bodies becomes
very weak. So astronauts in space are weightless. They float
like balloons in the air.

One way that astronauts become used to the **sensation** of
weightlessness is by flying in special planes. The planes climb
fast and come down fast. The astronauts feel weightless for a
few minutes. The planes do this **aerial** trick over and over.
Slowly the riders get used to the feeling of floating in space.
This training proved useful. Harris and astronaut Michael
Foale walked – and floated – in space for five hours!

★ Go back to the story. Underline the words or sentences that give
  you a clue to the meaning of each **boldfaced** word. ★

CONTEXT CLUES

Read each sentence. Look for clues to help you complete each sentence with a word or words from the box.

assignment	capsule	aerial	gravitational
dedicated	cockpit	commander	sensation
instructed	liftoff		

1. Dr. Bernard Harris, Jr., is a _____ astronaut who has spent many years in America's space program.

2. Dr. Harris was _____ by great teachers.

3. In 1995, his flight _____ was to ride in the space _____ on the shuttle *Discovery*.

4. Immediately after the *Discovery* countdown, there was the _____.

5. The _____ gave orders to the crew.

6. In space there is no _____ pull, so a person feels weightless.

7. Being weightless is a strange _____.

8. The *Discovery* crew steered the spaceship from the _____.

9. From space, the astronauts had a beautiful _____ view of Earth.

CHALLENGE YOURSELF

Name two things you might see in an aerial view of the earth.

_____   _____

Give two examples of a work assignment you have had.

_____   _____

SYNONYMS

Remember that **synonyms** are words that have the same or almost the same meaning. Read each underlined word on the left. Circle its synonym on the right.

1. dedicated   worried   devoted   finished

2. sensation   feeling   size   attitude

3. commander   building   chief   robot

4. instructed   promised   taught   related

5. assignment   help   pleasure   job

6. aerial   skyward   free   starry

WORD SENSE

Read each phrase. Check the Dictionary to see if the words make sense together. If they do, write yes on the line. If they do not, think of a word that does make sense with the underlined word. Write your word and the underlined word on the line.

1. gravitational boy _____

2. teacher instructed _____

3. confident commander _____

4. dedicated sandwich _____

5. purple sensation _____

6. difficult assignment _____

7. smiling capsule _____

8. smooth liftoff _____

9. curious cockpit _____

49

CROSSWORD PUZZLE

Use the clues and the words in the box to complete the crossword puzzle.

capsule	dedicated	cockpit	assignment
aerial	instructed	sensation	gravitational
liftoff	commander		

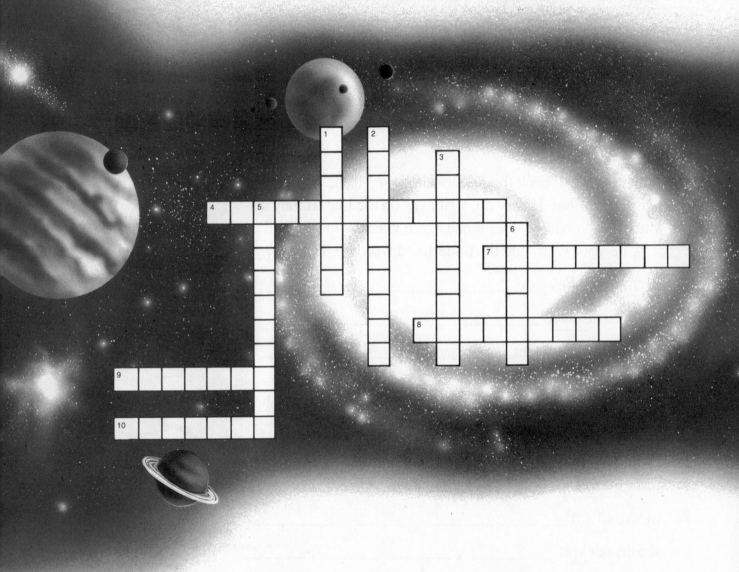

Across

4. related to gravity
7. loyal
8. leader
9. enclosed part of spacecraft
10. area where a pilot works

Down

1. the act of leaving the ground
2. taught
3. feeling
5. job to be carried out
6. in the air

Directions: Read the sentences. Look for the best word to use in the blank. Mark the answer space for your choice.

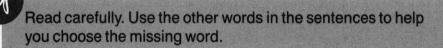

Tip

Read carefully. Use the other words in the sentences to help you choose the missing word.

1. The engines were fired. The spacecraft was ready for _____.
   Ⓐ assignment   Ⓒ liftoff
   Ⓑ capsule   Ⓓ messengers

2. The astronauts put on safety straps. They sat in the _____.
   Ⓕ capsule   Ⓗ kitchen
   Ⓖ commander   Ⓙ arena

3. Matt read about space. He did this for a class _____.
   Ⓐ assignment   Ⓒ sensation
   Ⓑ capsule   Ⓓ liftoff

4. The film taught about space travel. It _____ astronauts about flight.
   Ⓕ remembered   Ⓗ instructed
   Ⓖ dedicated   Ⓙ scolded

5. Anne told crew members what to do. She was the spacecraft _____.
   Ⓐ commander   Ⓒ capsule
   Ⓑ assignment   Ⓓ student

6. The astronauts flew safely. They controlled the shuttle from the _____.
   Ⓕ commander   Ⓗ liftoff
   Ⓖ cockpit   Ⓙ clouds

7. People float in space. This happens because there is no _____ pull.
   Ⓐ early   Ⓒ dedicated
   Ⓑ aerial   Ⓓ gravitational

8. The pictures of Earth were taken from the sky. They were _____ photographs.
   Ⓕ aerial   Ⓗ gravitational
   Ⓖ dedicated   Ⓙ narrow

9. The astronauts spent all their time studying space. They were _____ to their work.
   Ⓐ miserable   Ⓒ new
   Ⓑ dedicated   Ⓓ aerial

10. The feeling of having no weight occurs in space. This _____ makes some people uncomfortable.
    Ⓕ sensation   Ⓗ assignment
    Ⓖ cockpit   Ⓙ capsule

Writing

Imagine that you have the chance to fly on a space shuttle. Where would you like to go? What would you like to see? Remember that you would be weightless. How do you think it would feel?

On the lines below, tell about your space flight. What would you enjoy the most? What would you enjoy the least? Is there something special you would take with you? Use some vocabulary words in your writing.

Turn to "My Personal Word List" on page 131. Write some words from the story or other words that you would like to know more about. Use a dictionary to find the meanings.

★ To review the words in Lessons 5–8, turn to page 126. ★

SPORTS WATCH

From the Little League player to the Olympic star, sports are exciting for all who compete. Sports are also exciting to watch and to read about.

In Lessons 9–12, you will read about different sports and sports stars. Think about a sports event you went to or watched on television. Imagine the players in action. Were they lightning fast? Were they strong? Think about kinds of sports and the skills each requires. Write your ideas on the lines below.

Kinds of Sports	**Skills Needed**
_____	_____
_____	_____
_____	_____
_____	_____

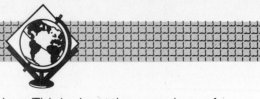

★ Read the story below. Think about the meanings of the **boldfaced** words. ★

Marvelous Jackie Robinson

Crack! Bat meets ball and Dodgers' Jackie Robinson quickly runs to third base. But the players on the other team cannot tag him out. So he steals home, scoring a run. Robinson is also **superb** while playing second base. He is such an excellent **fielder** that he can catch even the most difficult balls. Jackie Robinson is truly amazing!

In 1947, Robinson was named Rookie of the Year. In 1949, he won more **recognition**. He received the National League's Most Valuable Player award. Each year his **popularity** grew. Other players and millions of fans admired him. But Robinson's popularity was based on something more than **athletic** skill. He was the first black to play Major League baseball.

Before Robinson, there had been an unwritten rule that blacks could not play Major League baseball. Branch Rickey, the Dodgers' president, hated this rule. He felt it was very unfair. The rule made a **barrier** that shut fine players out of the game. To knock down this wall, he had to choose a very brave person. Jackie Robinson was the man he chose. Robinson was **courageous** enough to play a fine game even while hearing terrible insults. This required great determination and confidence.

Robinson knew about **prejudice**, about the unfair treatment of blacks and others. He wanted **equality** for blacks so they would be treated the same as whites. With guts and skill, Robinson was able to change things. His **influence** opened Major League sports to everyone.

★ Go back to the story. Underline the words or sentences that give you a clue to the meaning of each **boldfaced** word. ★

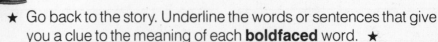

USING CONTEXT

Meanings for the vocabulary words are given below. Go back to the story and read each sentence that has a vocabulary word. If you still cannot tell the meaning, look for clues in the sentences that come before and after the one with the vocabulary word. Write each word in front of its meaning.

prejudice	barrier	fielder	courageous
influence	equality	superb	athletic
recognition	popularity		

1. _____ : an effect on other people or things

2. _____ : something that stands in the way

3. _____ : condition of being the same

4. _____ : brave

5. _____ : excellent; splendid

6. _____ : baseball player who plays around or outside the diamond

7. _____ : state of being liked by others

8. _____ : skilled at sport for which a person needs strength, ability, and speed

9. _____ : attention

10. _____ : opinion formed without knowing or caring about the facts

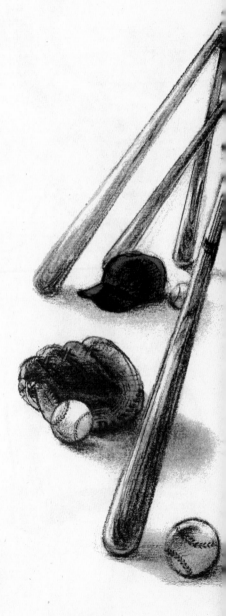

CHALLENGE YOURSELF

Name two people you consider <u>courageous</u>.

_____   _____

55

RELATED WORDS

Read each sentence. Find a word that is related to one of the words in the box. Underline the word in the sentence. Then write the word from the box on the line.

recognition	athletic	popularity
courageous	equality	superb

1. The story is about an athlete. _____

2. Did he recognize what lay ahead? _____

3. He was a popular player. _____

4. People admired his courage. _____

5. His skill was more than equal to that of other players. _____

6. He played baseball superbly. _____

WRITING SENTENCES

Use each vocabulary word in the box to write an original sentence.

influence	fielder	barrier
prejudice	superb	equality

1. _____

2. _____

3. _____

4. _____

5. _____

6. _____

TANGLED-UP WORDS

A word is underlined in each sentence below. The word sounds similar to a word in the box. But its meaning makes it the wrong word for the sentence.

Read the paragraphs. Find the word in the box that should replace the underlined word. Write the vocabulary word on the line next to the number of the underlined word.

recognition	equality	influence	barrier
fielder	athletic	superb	prejudice
courageous	popularity		

Jackie Robinson will be remembered for his (1) automatic ability. As a (2) feeler, he won many baseball awards. But his incredible (3) population comes from something else he did. He broke baseball's race (4) borrower. He believed that blacks and whites should have (5) quality. People admire what he did and say he was very (6) curious. He played a fine game in spite of terrible insults.

Jackie Robinson had an (7) endurance on baseball history. He was not only a (8) subway player. He spoke out against the (9) precious that kept him out of Major League baseball. His bravery and skill won him (10) permission forever. Fans will always remember marvelous Jackie Robinson.

1. _____   6. _____

2. _____   7. _____

3. _____   8. _____

4. _____   9. _____

5. _____   10. _____

GET WISE TO TESTS

Directions: Read the sentence or sentences. Look for the best word to use in the blank. Mark the answer space for your choice.

 Be sure to mark the answer space correctly. Do not mark the circle with an X or with a checkmark (✓). Instead, fill in the circle neatly and completely with your pencil.

1. She was an Olympic champion. She was _____ in field events.
   - Ⓐ superb
   - Ⓑ prejudiced
   - Ⓒ courageous
   - Ⓓ humorous

2. We all knew he worked hard. He won our _____.
   - Ⓕ prejudice
   - Ⓖ recognition
   - Ⓗ race
   - Ⓙ equality

3. Anyone can apply for the job. The company believes in _____.
   - Ⓐ influence
   - Ⓑ prejudice
   - Ⓒ limits
   - Ⓓ equality

4. He is the star of the team. He has strong _____ ability.
   - Ⓕ courageous
   - Ⓖ shining
   - Ⓗ recognition
   - Ⓙ athletic

5. The coach seems to show _____ by not letting girls play on the team.
   - Ⓐ promise
   - Ⓑ recognition
   - Ⓒ prejudice
   - Ⓓ equality

6. Everyone listens to what she says. Her _____ is strong.
   - Ⓕ influence
   - Ⓖ barrier
   - Ⓗ fielder
   - Ⓙ equality

7. They speak different languages. This creates a _____ between them.
   - Ⓐ recognition
   - Ⓑ beginning
   - Ⓒ fielder
   - Ⓓ barrier

8. Everyone likes Jan. Her _____ grows every year.
   - Ⓕ barrier
   - Ⓖ popularity
   - Ⓗ equality
   - Ⓙ doubt

9. The _____ lifeguard saved the drowning child.
   - Ⓐ hopeless
   - Ⓑ courageous
   - Ⓒ prejudice
   - Ⓓ foolish

10. He caught the high fly ball. He's a great _____.
    - Ⓕ fielder
    - Ⓖ barrier
    - Ⓗ climber
    - Ⓙ influence

Review

1. He _____ his free time to achieve his goal.
   - Ⓐ wasted
   - Ⓑ dedicated
   - Ⓒ ruined
   - Ⓓ instructed

2. The photo showed all the treetops. It was _____ view.
   - Ⓕ an aerial
   - Ⓖ a small
   - Ⓗ a muddy
   - Ⓙ an underwater

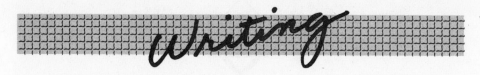
Writing

Jackie Robinson was a talented athlete. Yet for years he couldn't play Major League baseball because he was black. Do you know someone who has been treated unfairly?

Write a paragraph about what happened to that person. Tell how you felt about it. Use some vocabulary words in your writing.

_____

_____

_____

_____

_____

_____

_____

_____

_____

_____

_____

_____

_____

_____

_____

_____

Turn to "My Personal Word List" on page 132. Write some words from the story or other words that you would like to know more about. Use a dictionary to find the meanings.

59

★ Read the story below. Think about the meanings of the **boldfaced** words. ★

Athletes on Ice

Figure skating is the second most popular American sport. Why do you think it's such an attraction at the Winter Olympics?

Every four years, people look forward to the skating events of the Winter Olympics. Some people like the colorful costumes and artistic dance moves. Others appreciate the athletic skills and the feats of strength. Both men and women compete before a **panel** of judges in these exciting events. But it wasn't always this way.

In the early 1900s, women were not allowed to compete with men in world skating championships. For several years they were required to have their own separate figure-skating events. Then, in 1908, women were admitted to the Winter Olympics. Madge Sayers, a skater from Great Britain, won the first gold medal in women's figure skating.

Through the years, skaters have added their personal trademarks to the sport. Sonje Henie, the first world-renowned female skater, transformed the sport in the 1920s and 1930s with her beautiful ballet moves and her stunning appearance. In the 1960s, Peggy Fleming was given **credit** for bringing elegance and grace to the sport, and Dorothy Hamill's bubbly personality made her an instant American star in the 1970s.

Michelle Kwan's hard work and drive won the hearts of Americans in the 2002 Olympics. In that same year, young Sarah Hughes's breathtaking performance took the gold medal.

Figure skating got its name from the patterns or figures that the competitive skaters are required to make on the ice. As skaters twist and twirl, judges rate each **routine** for both technical and artistic form.

Skaters never seem to be satisfied with what they have done, and each year they attempt more complicated jumps and

Sonje Henie

spins. As their programs become harder and more daring, these athletes face the real prospect of being **injured.** An injury may keep a skater out of competition for a time. When this occurs, an **alternate** will have to step in to take the skater's place. Alternates, or substitute skaters, have trained hard and are ready to compete.

Athletes at the Olympics come from all over the world, and hail from places like Germany, France, Great Britain, the United States, and the **provinces** of Canada. They have passed skating tests at both a junior and a **senior** level, and they have placed at other major competitions, such as the U.S., European, or world championships.

Most successful skaters begin training when they are very young. Their **long-term** goal is to get good enough at the sport to win medals in skating competitions. Because they spend so much time training, young skaters often hire a private **tutor** to help them keep up with their schoolwork. These teachers may **quiz** their students in various subjects to make sure they are learning what they are supposed to.

The Olympic Games feature other types of skating besides figure skating. Men's speed skating dates back to 1924, and women's speed skating was added in 1960. Ice dancing, in which women and men compete in pairs, became an Olympic sport in 1976 and is gaining in popularity.

Figure skating is the most popular type of skating, however. That may be because adults are in awe of the skaters' abilities and children dream of becoming skating superstars someday.

Michelle Kwan

★ Go back to the story. Underline any words or sentences that give you clues to the meanings of the **boldfaced** words. ★

USING CONTEXT

Meanings for the vocabulary words are given below. Go back to the story and read each sentence that has a vocabulary word. If you still cannot tell the meaning, look for clues in the sentences that come before and after the one with the vocabulary word. Write each word in front of its meaning.

routine	provinces	alternate	long-term
injured	senior	panel	quiz
tutor	credit		

1. _____: hurt, damaged

2. _____: person who can take the place of another; substitute

3. _____: to question

4. _____: set of movements done over and over in same way

5. _____: lasting a long time

6. _____: advanced, higher; older

7. _____: recognition that a course of study has been completed

8. _____: big regions of a country

9. _____: private teacher

10. _____: a group of people chosen for a specific purpose

CHALLENGE YOURSELF

Name two <u>long-term</u> goals that you have.

_____   _____

Name two activities in which people perform <u>routines</u>.

_____   _____

MULTIPLE MEANINGS

The words in the box have more than one meaning. Look for clues in each sentence to tell which meaning is being used. Write the letter of the meaning next to the correct sentence.

quiz	routine
a. a test	**a.** a set of repeated movements
b. to question	**b.** ordinary, not special

_____ 1. Would you quiz me on the state capitals?

_____ 2. Lin did well on her math quiz.

_____ 3. I had a routine checkup.

_____ 4. Carlos included four leaps in his dance routine.

ANALOGIES

Remember that an **analogy** shows how two words go together in the same way as two other words. Write the words from the box to complete the following analogies.

long-term	provinces	alternate	quiz	panel
injured	senior	tutor	credit	

1. Higher is to lower as _____ is to junior.

2. Day is to night as _____ is to short-term.

3. Act is to behave as _____ is to ask.

4. Sad is to funny as _____ is to healthy.

5. Sections is to areas as _____ is to states.

6. Captain is to lead as _____ is to teach.

7. Image is to picture as _____ is to recognition.

8. Car is to auto as _____ is to substitute.

9. Alphabet is to letter as _____ is to person.

GET WISE TO TESTS

Directions: Choose the word or words that best take the place of the boldfaced word.

 Always read all the answer choices. Many choices may make sense, but only one answer choice has the same or almost the same meaning as the **boldfaced** word.

1. Each skater must perform a **routine** of moves. They have all practiced very hard.
   - Ⓐ distance
   - Ⓒ pattern
   - Ⓑ record
   - Ⓓ event

2. I want to make **long-term** plans. But for now, I'll make plans for the weekend.
   - Ⓕ easy
   - Ⓗ temporary
   - Ⓖ impressive
   - Ⓙ lasting

3. I didn't receive **credit** for the course. I was unable to finish it.
   - Ⓐ container
   - Ⓒ recognition
   - Ⓑ crevice
   - Ⓓ bill

4. Canada is made up of ten **provinces**. The United States is made up of 50 states.
   - Ⓕ neighbors
   - Ⓗ regions
   - Ⓖ promises
   - Ⓙ cities

5. She had a private **tutor** for her Spanish class. He helped her study.
   - Ⓐ performer
   - Ⓒ textbook
   - Ⓑ teacher
   - Ⓓ room

6. He was the **senior** officer in the department. He was in charge.
   - Ⓕ younger
   - Ⓗ shortest
   - Ⓖ taller
   - Ⓙ higher

7. You can be **injured** if you fall on the ice. You might even break a bone.
   - Ⓐ lost
   - Ⓒ hurt
   - Ⓑ caught
   - Ⓓ happy

8. We called in a **panel** of experts for help. We wanted advice from several people.
   - Ⓕ window
   - Ⓗ step
   - Ⓖ rope
   - Ⓙ group

9. We need to find an **alternate** to play in the game. Someone might get sick.
   - Ⓐ clever
   - Ⓒ substitute
   - Ⓑ willing
   - Ⓓ all-star

10. Please **quiz** me on this chapter of my science book. I have a test tomorrow.
    - Ⓕ question
    - Ⓗ decide
    - Ⓖ wonder
    - Ⓙ dismiss

Review

1. She is a **superb** skater. She can do anything on the ice.
   - Ⓐ terrible
   - Ⓒ good
   - Ⓑ excellent
   - Ⓓ poor

2. These teachers have a lot of **influence** on us. We follow their example.
   - Ⓕ effect
   - Ⓗ worries
   - Ⓖ friends
   - Ⓙ relatives

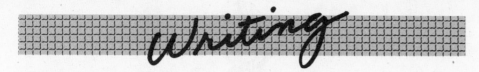
Writing

Imagine that a famous figure skater is coming to your town. You are chosen to interview the star for a newspaper story. You will be the person to ask her about all the things that everyone wants to know.

Think about what you and your readers would like to know about the star. Would you like to know where she was born, if she really enjoys practicing every day, and what she does to relax? Write five questions of your own for the interview. Use some vocabulary words in your writing.

1. _____

_____

_____

2. _____

_____

_____

3. _____

_____

_____

4. _____

_____

_____

Turn to "My Personal Word List" on page 132. Write some words from the story or other words that you would like to know more about. Use a dictionary to find the meanings.

5. _____

_____

_____

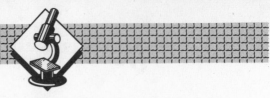

★ Read the story below. Think about the meanings of the **boldfaced** words. ★

Mind and Body

Two runners stand side by side at the starting line of a race. Both look very strong and fast. But one runner speeds ahead and wins the race. The other falls behind.

Some athletes can reach great goals such as the **achievement** of an Olympic gold medal. Others never live up to their promise. What kind of **preparation** before a race or other event makes the difference?

Everyone knows that athletes work out to **strengthen** their bodies. But **research** shows that strengthening the mind may be just as important. Careful study **indicates** that the best athletes win partly because they *think* they can win.

Thinking **positive** thoughts seems to give the edge for success in sports. People who say to themselves over and over, "I know I can do this," often find they have the **advantage** to win. On the other hand, people often fail who think, "I can't win."

One **procedure** that helps many athletes is creating pictures in the mind. They are told to think of each move they must make to win. Some use pictures that are more fanciful. One skater liked to imagine a star bursting inside her, filling her with energy. Another athlete who wanted to feel calm pictured himself as a bird floating in the air.

Next time you want to do something well, try training your mind to help you. Perhaps a teacher or other **instructor** can help you plan your training. If you imagine yourself doing better, you may soon see **improvement** in what you really can do. Positive thinking and pictures created in your mind can help you win!

★ Go back to the story. Underline the words or sentences that give you a clue to the meaning of each **boldfaced** word. ★

Using Context

Meanings for the vocabulary words are given below. Go back to the story and read each sentence that has a vocabulary word. If you still cannot tell the meaning, look for clues in the sentences that come before and after the one with the vocabulary word. Write each word in front of its meaning.

preparation	advantage	research	indicates
achievement	strengthen	instructor	improvement
positive	procedure		

1. _____ : something that is in your favor or helps

2. _____ : teacher

3. _____ : confident; sure

4. _____ : method of doing something

5. _____ : goal reached through skill or hard work

6. _____ : make stronger

7. _____ : points out; shows

8. _____ : careful study to find out facts

9. _____ : a change for the better; progress

10. _____ : making ready; something done to get ready

CHALLENGE YOURSELF

Name two activities in which <u>preparation</u> would help you.

_____   _____

Name two activities in which <u>positive</u> thoughts might help you.

_____   _____

WORD GROUPS

Read each pair of words. Think about how they are alike. Write the word from the box that best completes each group.

procedure	instructor	preparation
improvement	achievement	

1. gain, progress, _____

2. method, process, _____

3. teacher, leader, _____

4. feat, success, _____

5. plan, scheme, _____

CLOZE PARAGRAPH

Use the words in the box to complete the paragraph. Reread the paragraph to be sure it makes sense.

strengthen	positive	indicates
advantage	research	

    The expression on your face usually (1) _____ how you are already feeling. But (2) _____ shows that it can work the other way, too. You may be able to change your feelings by using "face flips." For example, an athlete might smile and look proud even if he or she is really feeling unsure. A (3) _____ expression on an athlete's face may improve the person's feelings and

(4) _____ his or her actions. This could provide the (5) _____ needed to win.

Directions: Read the phrase. Look for the word or words that have the same or almost the same meaning as the boldfaced word. Mark the answer space for your choice.

 This test will show how well you understand the meaning of the words. Think about the meaning of the **boldfaced** word before you choose your answer.

1. strong **advantage**
   - Ⓐ a soldier
   - Ⓑ a help
   - Ⓒ an adventure
   - Ⓓ a feeling

2. follow a **procedure**
   - Ⓕ leader
   - Ⓖ preparation
   - Ⓗ highway
   - Ⓙ method

3. **improvement** in reading
   - Ⓐ instructor
   - Ⓑ progress
   - Ⓒ procedure
   - Ⓓ imagination

4. her greatest **achievement**
   - Ⓕ assignment to a job
   - Ⓖ desire
   - Ⓗ success at a goal
   - Ⓙ problem

5. the map **indicates**
   - Ⓐ shows
   - Ⓑ needs
   - Ⓒ grows
   - Ⓓ inspects

6. a good **instructor**
   - Ⓕ improvement
   - Ⓖ detective
   - Ⓗ direction
   - Ⓙ teacher

7. careful **research**
   - Ⓐ study
   - Ⓑ encyclopedias
   - Ⓒ procedure
   - Ⓓ writing

8. to **strengthen** a team
   - Ⓕ research
   - Ⓖ make comments about
   - Ⓗ make stronger
   - Ⓙ break up

9. a **positive** feeling
   - Ⓐ helpless
   - Ⓑ confident
   - Ⓒ possible
   - Ⓓ forgetful

10. **preparation** for a race
   - Ⓕ starter
   - Ⓖ research
   - Ⓗ program
   - Ⓙ training

Review

1. **commander** of the crew
   - Ⓐ assignment
   - Ⓑ instructor
   - Ⓒ guest
   - Ⓓ leader

2. **superb** ability
   - Ⓕ excellent
   - Ⓖ new
   - Ⓗ positive
   - Ⓙ weak

3. **species** of birds
   - Ⓐ songs
   - Ⓑ kinds
   - Ⓒ eyesight
   - Ⓓ feat

4. **courageous** pilot
   - Ⓕ curious
   - Ⓖ brave
   - Ⓗ popular
   - Ⓙ lost

5. avoid **prejudice**
   - Ⓐ accidents
   - Ⓑ equality
   - Ⓒ recognition
   - Ⓓ unfairness

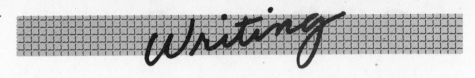

As you have read, many athletes create pictures in their minds to help them succeed. Think about being a runner or skater.

Write a paragraph describing the pictures, or images, you would create to help you succeed. Explain how they would help you win a race or skate more gracefully without falls. Use some vocabulary words in your writing.

I am a _____ and I want to do my best. So I create pictures in my mind to help me. One picture

I create _____

_____

_____

_____

_____

_____

_____

_____

_____

_____

_____

_____

_____

_____

_____

_____

Turn to "My Personal Word List" on page 132. Write some words from the story or other words that you would like to know more about. Use a dictionary to find the meanings.

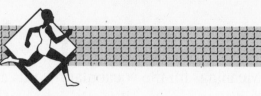

★ Read the story below. Think about the meanings of the **boldfaced** words. ★

She's Really on the Ball!

It is half time at the basketball game. Suddenly, Tanya Crevier is on the court. She begins juggling basketballs – four of them at once!

Then Crevier seeks a helper from the audience. As he comes forward, she grabs a baby bib and a can of soda. In careful, **precise** movements, she ties the bib around his neck. Then she spins the ball on the edge of the can. At the same time, she pours the drink into the helper's mouth.

The crowd goes wild, but the **exhibition** is just beginning. What a show! Crevier grabs three balls and dribbles all of them at the same time, up and down the court. Then she is ready for the next step in her **sequence** of tricks. She sits down and puts straps and a brace on her feet. In a moment, she is spinning nine basketballs at the same time. This trick requires **considerable** athletic skill. But it's no problem for Crevier. She has a great deal of ability.

Crevier practices hard. She knows that **rigorous** training helps her keep her skills. It helps her **maintain** her speed and control. She also knows that training requires a lot of **discipline**, or willpower.

Crevier was a star, an **outstanding** athlete, in high school and college. Now she does hundreds of shows a year. But the tricks done by this appealing performer are not the only part of her show. Once the **attractive** and lively athlete has a group's attention, she talks to them. She talks about enthusiasm and about always trying hard. She talks about having confidence. Being a positive role model is not an extra feature of Crevier's show. It is an **essential** part. Tanya Crevier uses her skills to make a difference in people's lives.

★ Go back to the story. Underline the words or sentences that give you a clue to the meaning of each **boldfaced** word. ★

USING CONTEXT

Meanings for the vocabulary words are given below. Go back to the story and read each sentence that has a vocabulary word. If you still cannot tell the meaning, look for clues in the sentences that come before and after the one with the vocabulary word. Write each word in front of its meaning.

precise	essential	exhibition	discipline
sequence	attractive	rigorous	outstanding
maintain	considerable		

1. _____: difficult, strict

2. _____: necessary

3. _____: exact, very careful

4. _____: training and self-control

5. _____: to keep up or keep the same

6. _____: a great deal; much

7. _____: a show; display

8. _____: standing out; better than others

9. _____: one thing following another

10. _____: pleasing

CHALLENGE YOURSELF

Name two things that are essential to life.

_____   _____

Name two things you do in a sequence each morning.

_____   _____

WORD GROUPS

Read each pair of words. Think about how they are alike.
Write the word from the box that best completes each group.

outstanding	discipline	precise	rigorous
considerable	exhibition	attractive	essential
sequence	maintain		

1. much, large, _____

2. keep up, preserve, _____

3. pretty, handsome, _____

4. display, show, _____

5. necessary, required, _____

6. difficult, demanding, _____

7. finest, best, _____

8. training, self-control, _____

9. order, series, _____

10. exact, accurate, _____

WORD ORIGINS

A **word origin** is the history of a word. Knowing where a
word comes from can help you understand its meaning.
Read each word origin. Then write each word from the box
in front of its origin.

rigorous	discipline	sequence

1. _____ : from Latin sequentia, that which
follows

2. _____ : from Middle English rigour,
hardship

3. _____ : from Latin discipulus, pupil

WORD SENSE

Read each phrase. Check the Dictionary to see if the words make sense together. If they do, write <u>yes</u> on the line. If they do not, think of a word that does make sense with the underlined word. Write your word and the underlined word on the line.

1. <u>essential</u> details _____

2. <u>attractive</u> monster _____

3. <u>maintain</u> quality _____

4. <u>outstanding</u> results _____

5. <u>invisible</u> exhibition _____

6. <u>rigorous</u> relaxation _____

7. <u>precise</u> schedule _____

WRITING SENTENCES

Use each vocabulary word in the box to write an original sentence.

essential	outstanding	discipline	sequence
precise	attractive	considerable	

1. _____

2. _____

3. _____

4. _____

5. _____

6. _____

7. _____

Directions: Read the phrase. Look for the word or words that have the same or almost the same meaning as the boldfaced word. Mark the answer space for your choice.

Always read all the answer choices. Many choices may make sense. But only one answer choice has the same or almost the same meaning as the **boldfaced word.**

1. **considerable** skill
   - Ⓐ small
   - Ⓒ great
   - Ⓑ considerate
   - Ⓓ missing

2. **attractive** child
   - Ⓕ pretty
   - Ⓗ precise
   - Ⓖ well-behaved
   - Ⓙ attentive

3. exact **sequence**
   - Ⓐ skill
   - Ⓒ location
   - Ⓑ offer
   - Ⓓ order

4. artist's **exhibition**
   - Ⓕ lack
   - Ⓗ show
   - Ⓖ talent
   - Ⓙ training

5. **precise** schedule
   - Ⓐ prepared
   - Ⓒ relaxed
   - Ⓑ exact
   - Ⓓ sloppy

6. **maintain** skills
   - Ⓕ keep up
   - Ⓗ look for
   - Ⓖ reveal
   - Ⓙ request

7. athlete's **discipline**
   - Ⓐ self-control
   - Ⓒ confidence
   - Ⓑ energy
   - Ⓓ laziness

8. **essential** items
   - Ⓕ many
   - Ⓗ necessary
   - Ⓖ useless
   - Ⓙ excellent

9. **rigorous** training
   - Ⓐ easy
   - Ⓒ rapid
   - Ⓑ strict
   - Ⓓ half-hearted

10. **outstanding** performer
    - Ⓕ late
    - Ⓗ important
    - Ⓖ too tall
    - Ⓙ better than others

Review

1. skills **advantage**
   - Ⓐ disability
   - Ⓒ comfort
   - Ⓑ helpful edge
   - Ⓓ too loud

2. **strengthen** muscles
   - Ⓕ make stronger
   - Ⓗ make weaker
   - Ⓖ lengthen
   - Ⓙ save

3. golf **instructor**
   - Ⓐ helper
   - Ⓒ course
   - Ⓑ equipment
   - Ⓓ teacher

4. **positive** attitude
   - Ⓕ confident
   - Ⓗ jealous
   - Ⓖ electric
   - Ⓙ fearful

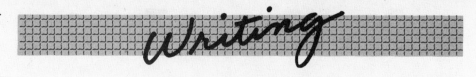

Tanya Crevier is famous for her skill in performing basketball tricks. Do you have a favorite skill or activity? Think about what you enjoy doing most in your spare time. Now imagine giving a performance for your friends. What skills would you "show off" for your audience?

Describe your imaginary performance. Also tell how you learned your skills and why you like them. Use some vocabulary words in your writing.

_____

_____

_____

_____

_____

_____

_____

_____

_____

_____

_____

_____

_____

_____

_____

_____

Turn to "My Personal Word List" on page 132. Write some words from the story or other words that you would like to know more about. Use a dictionary to find the meanings.

★ To review the words in Lessons 9–12, turn to page 127. ★

SMALL WORLDS

We share our planet with many small creatures. Some work together as a team, and some work alone. Some spin webs. Others make honey. These small creatures perform many different tasks.

In Lessons 13–16, you will read about different kinds of small creatures. Think about some you have seen. Which ones have eight legs? Which ones fly? Which ones crawl? On the lines below, list some names of small creatures and what you know about them.

Names of Small Creatures	About the Small Creatures

★ Read the story below. Think about the meanings of the **boldfaced** words. ★

A Well-Ordered World

You're walking up a hill and stop to catch your breath. You look down and see ants scurrying in all different directions. It looks as if the ants don't know what they are doing or where they are going. Yet, ants have a very well-ordered world.

Within the **organization** of an ant colony, each ant has a job to do. Each colony has thousands of worker ants and one or more queen ants. Worker ants build the nest, find food, and take care of young ants. Groups **cooperate** on many tasks. They hurry and **bustle** about to help one another complete the work. At the center of their lives is the queen.

People have admired the well-ordered world of ants. They have wished that humans would cooperate as well as ants. Thousands of ants are crowded together in a **teeming** nest. Yet, they never fight each other. They fight only when there is an outside **threat**. Then they **defend** the nest against attack.

The worker ants accept the **authority** of the queen. The queen has a special way of giving orders. Her body makes a chemical on her skin that worker ants lick. Ants seem to like its taste. It makes them act in certain ways. It gives them orders. They pass the chemical and its messages on to other ants.

Young ants also have a chemical that sends messages or orders to adult worker ants. The worker ants like the taste of this chemical, too. Their orders are to feed and groom the young ants. Workers never seem to tire of caring for them. Their **tireless** care makes sure that the young ants grow up to be healthy. When the young ants reach **adulthood**, they become, in turn, worker ants.

The nest's **existence** depends on workers caring for the queen and the young ants. Nature programs ants to do particular kinds of jobs and this makes for their well-ordered world.

★ Go back to the story. Underline the words or sentences that give you a clue to the meaning of each **boldfaced** word. ★

USING CONTEXT

Meanings for the vocabulary words are given below. Go back to the story and read each sentence that has a vocabulary word. If you still cannot tell the meaning, look for clues in the sentences that come before and after the one with the vocabulary word. Write each word in front of its meaning.

cooperate	tireless	teeming	authority
organization	defend	threat	existence
adulthood	bustle		

1. _____ : group that has a common purpose

2. _____ : condition of being grown-up

3. _____ : to be noisy and busy

4. _____ : full of life; swarming

5. _____ : not needing rest

6. _____ : to work together

7. _____ : a state of being

8. _____ : power to command

9. _____ : signal that harm will occur

10. _____ : to keep safe; protect

CHALLENGE YOURSELF

Name two <u>organizations</u> you belong to or know something about.

_____   _____

Name two people of <u>authority</u> that you know.

_____   _____

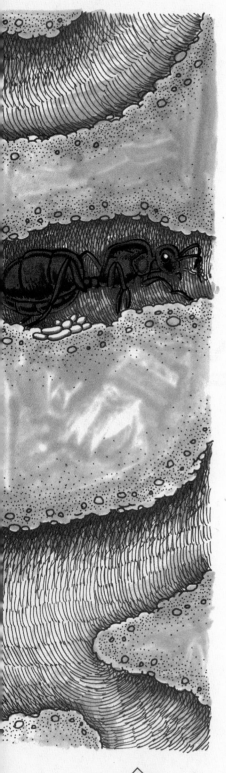

WRITING SENTENCES

Use each vocabulary word in the box to write an original sentence.

existence	adulthood	tireless	organization

1. _____

2. _____

3. _____

4. _____

CLOZE PARAGRAPH

Use the words in the box to complete the paragraphs. Reread the paragraphs to be sure they make sense.

threat	bustle	cooperate	authority
teeming	defend		

Can ants (1) _____ themselves successfully?

When another insect or other animal becomes a

(2) _____ to a fire ant, the fire ant stings. Other

kinds of ants also refuse to (3) _____ with their

enemies, and they spray a liquid or bite to discourage the enemy

from moving any closer.

Most ant colonies are (4) _____ with worker

ants. They (5) _____ around their colony and

work rather than fight. From whom do they get their orders?

The queen has complete (6) _____.

WORD MAP

Use the vocabulary words in the box to complete the word map about ant colonies. Add other words that you know to each group.

tireless	defend	bustle
organization	cooperate	authority

Jobs of Worker Ants

1. _____
2. _____
3. _____
4. _____
5. _____

Ways Ants Act

1. _____
2. _____
3. _____
4. _____
5. _____

ANT COLONY

About the Ant Colony Queen

1. _____
2. _____
3. _____
4. _____

GET WISE TO TESTS

Directions: Read each sentence. Pick the word that best completes the sentence. Mark the answer space for that word.

 Before you choose your answer, try reading the sentence with each answer choice. This will help you choose an answer that makes sense.

1. The teenager looked forward to _____.
   Ⓐ confusing   Ⓒ adulthood
   Ⓑ threat   Ⓓ yesterday

2. The _____ workers finished the job.
   Ⓕ cooperate   Ⓗ about
   Ⓖ tireless   Ⓙ expand

3. The bees _____ about from flower to flower.
   Ⓐ commander   Ⓒ defend
   Ⓑ bustle   Ⓓ sky

4. A _____ crowd cheered the players.
   Ⓕ quickly   Ⓗ defend
   Ⓖ silent   Ⓙ teeming

5. We will _____ to get the job done.
   Ⓐ cooperate   Ⓒ lamb
   Ⓑ waste   Ⓓ authority

6. His _____ frightened us.
   Ⓕ adulthood   Ⓗ threat
   Ⓖ friendly   Ⓙ vaguely

7. Our principal has the _____ to make rules.
   Ⓐ existence   Ⓒ authority
   Ⓑ polite   Ⓓ newspaper

8. It's fun to be a member of a good _____.
   Ⓕ organization   Ⓗ teeming
   Ⓖ existence   Ⓙ positive

9. Can you _____ your strange ideas?
   Ⓐ taste   Ⓒ lifelike
   Ⓑ defend   Ⓓ cooperate

10. The ant colony's _____ depends on the queen.
    Ⓕ tireless   Ⓗ flipper
    Ⓖ without   Ⓙ existence

Review

1. The directions were clear and _____.
   Ⓐ outstanding   Ⓒ close
   Ⓑ actions   Ⓓ precise

2. The _____ training made her a winner.
   Ⓕ performed   Ⓗ maintain
   Ⓖ rigorous   Ⓙ strength

3. Sleep is _____ to good health.
   Ⓐ essential   Ⓒ not required
   Ⓑ rested   Ⓓ attractive

4. Arrange the numbers in _____.
   Ⓕ sequence   Ⓗ helpful
   Ⓖ clear   Ⓙ discipline

Writing

Science-fiction writers often set their stories in other worlds. Begin a science-fiction story. Imagine that you have become small enough to visit the world of an ant colony. You explore the rooms in a nest and watch the ants' activities.

　　Write your story about what you see and do. Use the picture to help you describe what happens to you. Use some vocabulary words in your writing.

　　Down, down, and down I went into the ant colony. _____

_____

_____

_____

_____

_____

_____

_____

_____

_____

_____

_____

_____

_____

_____

_____

_____

Turn to "My Personal Word List" on page 132. Write some words from the story or other words that you would like to know more about. Use a dictionary to find the meanings.

★ Read the story below. Think about the meanings of the **boldfaced** words. ★

The Prophet and the Spider

This Arabian tale explains why some people say it is good luck not to kill a spider.

As a **caravan** driver, Mohammed was wise in the ways of following the salt trails and camel tracks. But he and his friend, Abu, had gone only a few miles when a sandstorm suddenly swept about them. The whirlwind flung sand in their faces, stinging their eyes and filling their throats with **grit**. It blotted out the blazing sun above their hands and erased the path before their feet. With neither bush nor tree for a **landmark**, Mohammed and his merchant friend were lost.

Then, muffled by the shrieking of the storm, they heard the snorting of horses. Mohammed's enemies had discovered his escape and had come in **pursuit**. Mohammed dropped to his knees and asked Allah for help. Almost at once the wind died and the sand **sifted** back to the ground. When Mohammed lifted his eyes he noticed a large outcropping of rock. Between two huge boulders was a narrow opening.

"See, my friend?" Mohammed pointed. "Allah is watching out for us, for there is our **haven**."

"There is not time!" Abu cried. Turning, he saw the rocks and shook his head. "Nor is there room enough."

Mohammed walked calmly to the rock and pushed his forefinger against it. Although the stone weighed many tons, it shifted beneath his touch as if it were no bigger than a pebble. The boulder slid aside until the opening was wide enough for Mohammed to slip within.

Between the rocks was a small dark cave. The cave was home for a great many eight-legged and six-legged and four-legged and no-legged creatures as well. As soon as Mohammed and Abu crowded in, scorpions and beetles and lizards and snakes **scuttled** and slithered from the cave. Only a single great spider remained, suspended from a slender strand

above Mohammed's head.

Abu Bakr shuddered when he saw the spider and swung his goatskin bag at the web.

Mohammed caught his arm. "No," he commanded. "To Allah belongs everyone **dwelling** in the heavens and on earth."

Outside the cave they could clearly hear men's voices. They sat still as the stones surrounding them. Only the spider moved. Back and forth, up and down, the spider strung its spokes until a **mesh** completely covered the entrance.

Then they heard someone shout, "Look, there are fresh tracks in the sand — and this rock has been shifted!"

"You, there, boy!" a different voice ordered. "You are slight enough to crawl in that cave. Take a look!"

"Please, Agha, I cannot!" A shadow fell across the cave's entrance, and a trembling voice added, "A huge and hairy spider is hanging there."

"How could Mohammed be inside, then?" asked another. "He would surely have broken this web and frightened the spider."

"You are right." It was the man who had spoken first. "This web has not been disturbed. Mohammed cannot be concealed in the grotto."

"Then he must be ahead of us," said still another.

There was the scramble and shouting of men remounting their horses, and once again the sand shook from pounding hooves.

Mohammed looked at the spider, **silhouetted** against the light that slanted in between the boulders. It sat quietly in the center of its great web like the sun in the sky, surrounded by rays. Mohammed touched his forehead to the floor. "Thank Allah, Abu Bakr, for thus delivering us from danger."

When they were certain that their enemies had given up pursuit, Mohammed and Abu Bakr continued their journey. Because of a spider, the life of the Prophet had been saved. And that is why his followers still spare a spider's life, even today.

From Someone Saw a Spider, Spider Facts and Folktales, by Shirley Climo

★ Go back to the story. Underline any words or sentences that give you clues to the meanings of the **boldfaced** words. ★

CONTEXT CLUES

Read each sentence below. Choose a word from the box that means the same as the underlined part of each sentence. Write the word on the line after the sentence.

dwelling	haven	landmark	silhouetted
pursuit	grit	caravan	scuttled
sifted	mesh		

1. Mohammed knew the desert because he had often crossed it with a <u>group of people traveling together for safety</u>. _____

2. He knew that he would not find a tree or another <u>familiar object that guides the way</u>. _____

3. He watched as the hot sun <u>showed the outline of his body</u> on the sand. _____

4. He was stopped by a swirling sandstorm that blinded him in a sea of <u>very fine bits of sand</u>. _____

5. Then, when the wind quieted down, the sand <u>fell lightly</u> to the ground. _____

6. The people who were involved in the <u>chase</u> of Mohammed knew the desert, too. _____

7. But they did not know that Mohammed would find a <u>place of shelter and safety</u> in a cave. _____

8. Many creatures were <u>making their home</u> in the cave, including a spider. _____

9. Most of the creatures <u>ran quickly</u> away when Mohammed and his friend entered the cave. _____

10. Only the spider stayed, to spin a fine <u>weaving with open spaces</u> that saved Mohammed's life. _____

MULTIPLE MEANINGS

The words in the box have more than one meaning. Look for clues in each sentence to tell which meaning is being used. Write the letter of the meaning next to the correct sentence.

landmark	grit
a. familiar object used as a guide	**a.** very fine bits of gravel or sand
b. an important event	**b.** courage

_____ **1.** That rock is a <u>landmark</u> used by many hikers.

_____ **2.** It was a <u>landmark</u> discovery.

_____ **3.** He is a hero with true <u>grit</u>.

_____ **4.** The wind blew <u>grit</u> in my eye.

CLOZE PARAGRAPH

Use the words in the box to complete the paragraphs. Reread the paragraphs to be sure they make sense.

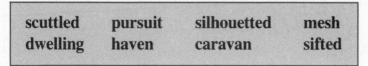

scuttled	pursuit	silhouetted	mesh
dwelling	haven	caravan	sifted

The people in a (1) _____ crossing the desert

were often merchants. They traveled in (2) _____

of riches, like cloth made of gold (3) _____.

The trip was difficult. For hundreds of miles they would see

only huge sand dunes (4) _____ against the sky.

Blowing sand (5) _____ onto their bodies.

Scorpions (6) _____ across their path. Other

creatures (7) _____ in the desert might also
sting or bite. Fortunately, they would find an occasional

watering hole, a (8) _____ in a hot, dry land.

GET WISE TO TESTS

Directions: Read each sentence. Pick the word that best completes the sentence. Mark the answer space for that word.

Tip

If you are not sure which word completes the sentence, do the best you can. Try to choose the answer that makes the most sense.

1. The chairs in the basement were covered with _____.
   - Ⓐ pursuit
   - Ⓒ grit
   - Ⓑ sky
   - Ⓓ sandy

2. You could see the tree _____ against the garage door.
   - Ⓕ around
   - Ⓗ sifted
   - Ⓖ silhouetted
   - Ⓙ seated

3. _____ near the sea makes many people very happy.
   - Ⓐ Dwelling
   - Ⓒ Pinching
   - Ⓑ Handsome
   - Ⓓ Scuttled

4. A fine _____ protected the plants from insects.
   - Ⓕ landmark
   - Ⓗ triumph
   - Ⓖ inferior
   - Ⓙ mesh

5. Grains of sand _____ from his hand to the ground.
   - Ⓐ sang
   - Ⓒ sculpture
   - Ⓑ sifted
   - Ⓓ caravan

6. Our courthouse is a town _____.
   - Ⓕ landmark
   - Ⓗ caravan
   - Ⓖ relating
   - Ⓙ recipe

7. The beach hut became a _____ from the rain.
   - Ⓐ grit
   - Ⓒ message
   - Ⓑ noisy
   - Ⓓ haven

8. The _____ transported goods across the desert.
   - Ⓕ haven
   - Ⓗ icy
   - Ⓖ caravan
   - Ⓙ excuse

9. The spider _____ to the center of its web.
   - Ⓐ homework
   - Ⓒ scuttled
   - Ⓑ landmark
   - Ⓓ divided

10. The hikers were in _____ of a rare bird.
    - Ⓕ mesh
    - Ⓗ pursuit
    - Ⓖ lonely
    - Ⓙ refrain

Review

1. I hope we can all work together and _____ to get this job done.
   - Ⓐ cooperate
   - Ⓒ finished
   - Ⓑ trying
   - Ⓓ fight

2. He is a _____ worker who is always ready to help.
   - Ⓕ lazy
   - Ⓗ tireless
   - Ⓖ sleeper
   - Ⓙ sadly

Writing

Mohammed's friend, Abu Bakr, was afraid of the spider in the cave. If Mohammed had not stopped him, he would have killed the spider, even though it had not tried to bite them. People are sometimes afraid of spiders or other creatures without good reason.

Think about an animal that you or someone you know is afraid of. On the lines below, tell why this animal is frightening. Then tell why the fears about this animal are unnecessary. Use some vocabulary words in your writing.

Turn to "My Personal Word List" on page 132. Write some words from the story or other words that you would like to know more about. Use a dictionary to find the meanings.

★ Read the story below. Think about the meanings of the **boldfaced** words. ★

Insect Self-Defense

Many insects end their short lives as the **victims** of other animals. Birds and fish hunt insects. Frogs, snakes, spiders, and bats **devour** them by the millions. Insects, of course, do not want to be eaten alive. So nature has given them a number of ways to stay away from their enemies.

Small insects often **conceal** themselves for safety. During the day, they hide in dark, secret places. At night, they come out to eat. This **behavior**, or way of acting, makes it less likely that enemies will spot them.

Other insects can hide right out in the open. Some moths, for example, are colored just like tree bark. Stick-insects look like twigs. Leaf-insects are flat and green. As long as these insects do not move, they are hard to find in nature. Once they move, however, they may **attract** an enemy.

Bees do not need to hide. They **specialize** in attacking their enemies. A small animal can be **paralyzed**, or made unable to move, by a bee sting.

Some insects are **poisonous**. Birds that eat and **digest** such insects become sick. So they learn to become more **attentive** to what they eat. They know which insects to avoid.

Insects have many ways of defending themselves in nature. They know how to hide so their enemies do not see them. They can attack or paralyze their enemies. They can even change their bodies to be less attractive to their enemies. But the most important way of protecting themselves is by having many offspring. Insects multiply by the millions. Then, no matter how many are eaten, their numbers remain about the same.

★ Go back to the story. Underline the words or sentences that give you a clue to the meaning of each **boldfaced** word. ★

USING CONTEXT

Meanings for the vocabulary words are given below. Go back to the story and read each sentence that has a vocabulary word. If you still cannot tell the meaning, look for clues in the sentences that come before and after the one with the vocabulary word. Write each word in front of its meaning.

victims	behavior	paralyzed	digest
devour	specialize	poisonous	attentive
conceal	attract		

1. _____ : a way of acting

2. _____ : involved in one branch of work

3. _____ : animals or people hurt or destroyed

4. _____ : to eat hungrily

5. _____ : hide

6. _____ : to gain attention

7. _____ : containing harmful poison

8. _____ : change food in the body for the use of the body

9. _____ : unable to move or feel

10. _____ : alert; aware of

CHALLENGE YOURSELF

Name two animals or plants that can be poisonous.

_____   _____

Name two foods you like to devour.

_____   _____

WORD GROUPS

Read each pair of words. Think about how they are alike. Write the word from the box that best completes each group.

devour	paralyzed	poisonous	attract
attentive	behavior	conceal	

1. harmful, deadly, _____

2. eat, taste, _____

3. hide, cover, _____

4. actions, manner, _____

5. watchful, alert, _____

6. frozen, motionless, _____

7. invite, lure, _____

WORD SENSE

Read each phrase. Check the Dictionary to see if the words make sense together. If they do, write yes on the line. If they do not, think of a word that does make sense with the underlined word. Write your word and the underlined word on the line.

1. digest table _____

2. busy victims _____

3. specialize in medicine _____

4. attract attention _____

5. paralyzed laugh _____

6. attentive sleeper _____

7. poisonous spider _____

Directions: Read the sentences. Look for the best word to use in the blank. Mark the answer space for your choice.

Tip Read carefully. Use the other words in the sentences to help you choose the missing word.

1. Stay away from rattlesnakes. Their bite is _____.
   Ⓐ happy   Ⓒ harmless
   Ⓑ full   Ⓓ poisonous

2. The dog had not eaten for days. He began to _____ the food.
   Ⓕ specialize   Ⓗ write
   Ⓖ devour   Ⓙ give

3. I collect stamps from all over the world. However, I _____ in stamps from France.
   Ⓐ think   Ⓒ specialize
   Ⓑ digest   Ⓓ imagine

4. She always listens very carefully in class. She is very _____.
   Ⓕ attentive   Ⓗ poisonous
   Ⓖ foolish   Ⓙ lonely

5. Hide this present. I want to _____ it from my friend.
   Ⓐ conceal   Ⓒ borrow
   Ⓑ attract   Ⓓ divide

6. Cover the bowl. The sugar will _____ the bees.
   Ⓕ digest   Ⓗ conceal
   Ⓖ split   Ⓙ attract

7. The boy could not move his legs after the accident. They were _____.
   Ⓐ paralyzed   Ⓒ repeated
   Ⓑ designed   Ⓓ attentive

8. Wolves run in packs. They run after and attack their _____.
   Ⓕ behavior   Ⓗ victims
   Ⓖ voices   Ⓙ driveways

9. Don't swim right after you eat. You need time to _____ your food.
   Ⓐ specialize   Ⓒ attract
   Ⓑ digest   Ⓓ entertain

10. The students were orderly during the fire drill. Their teachers were impressed with their _____.
    Ⓕ childhood   Ⓗ victims
    Ⓖ handwriting   Ⓙ behavior

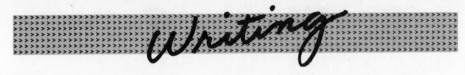

Writing

Insects have different ways of defending themselves. Some, like bees, attack their enemies while others, like the praying mantis, have special ways of concealing themselves.

Write a paragraph discussing both types of insect defense. Which method do you think is more effective? Give reasons for your opinion. Use some vocabulary words in your writing.

Turn to "My Personal Word List" on page 132. Write some words from the story or other words that you would like to know more about. Use a dictionary to find the meanings.

★ Read the story below. Think about the meanings of the **boldfaced** words. ★

Spiders Are Builders

You are trapped in a giant sticky net. A hairy monster appears and surrounds you. Its eight legs **encircle** you. This might sound like a bad dream to you. But it happens every night to millions of insects.

The monster is a spider, and the net is its web. To us, spider webs are **fragile**. But the webs are strong enough to hold most insects. Because the webs are **flexible**, they can bend to hold trapped insects in place.

A spider spins a web by letting out liquid silk from its body. The liquid dries and forms a thread. The spider ties one end of the silk to a wall or a tree. Then it **suspends** itself from the thread. As the spider hangs, the thread gets longer. A completed web might be made up of dozens of silk threads.

Spiders spin webs in many different shapes. The most common is **circular**, like a dinner plate. The web has threads that go from its center to its edges. The **diameter**, the distance across the web, may be as great as two feet.

Spiders also spin webs shaped like **rectangles**. These four-sided webs have **vertical** threads that run up and down. They also have **horizontal** threads running from side to side. These threads combine to form a kind of net. The net is used to catch insects for the spider to eat.

The web most people know is often seen in the corners of ceilings. These webs sometimes get tangled and collect dust. When that happens, they are known as **cobwebs**. You are not likely to find a spider in a cobweb. A cobweb is not very useful. The spider cannot pull on the threads to catch insects. So it goes off to form another web, one that will help it get food.

★ Go back to the story. Underline the words or sentences that give you a clue to the meaning of each **boldfaced** word. ★

USING CONTEXT

Meanings for the vocabulary words are given below. Go back to the story and read each sentence that has a vocabulary word. If you still cannot tell the meaning, look for clues in the sentences that come before and after the one with the vocabulary word. Write each word in front of its meaning.

fragile	circular	cobwebs	suspends
encircle	flexible	diameter	rectangles
vertical	horizontal		

1. _____ : in the same direction as the horizon

2. _____ : to form a circle around something

3. _____ : webs no longer used by spiders

4. _____ : easily destroyed

5. _____ : a line that goes from one side of a circle to another, passing through the center point

6. _____ : hangs

7. _____ : straight up and down

8. _____ : in the shape of a circle

9. _____ : four-sided shapes with four right angles and two sides that are longer than the other two

10. _____ : bends easily

CHALLENGE YOURSELF

Name two things that are <u>fragile</u>.

_____

Name two things that you can <u>suspend</u> from the ceiling.

_____

ANALOGIES

An **analogy** shows how two words go together in the same way as two other words. Write the words from the box to complete the following analogies.

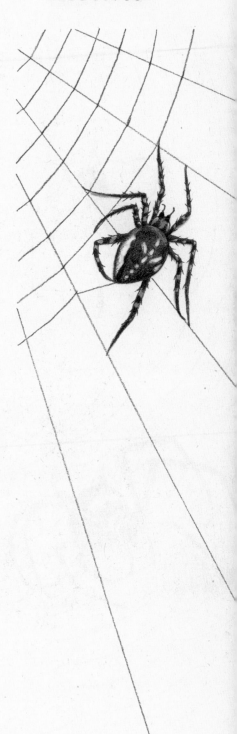

suspends	fragile	circular
cobwebs	flexible	rectangles

1. Steel is to strong as glass is to _____.

2. Buildings are to ruins as spider webs are to _____.

3. Balls are to circles as cartons are to _____.

4. Straight is to bent as stiff is to _____.

5. Four-sided is to square as round is to _____.

6. Leaps is to jumps as hangs is to _____.

WRITING SENTENCES

Use each vocabulary word in the box to write an original sentence.

encircle	suspends	vertical	fragile
diameter	horizontal	circular	flexible

1. _____

2. _____

3. _____

4. _____

5. _____

6. _____

7. _____

8. _____

HIDDEN MESSAGE PUZZLE

Write a word from the box next to each clue. To find the message, copy the numbered letters in the matching numbered boxes at the bottom of the page. Then you will know why spiders play in the outfield.

vertical	rectangles	encircle	fragile
flexible	suspends	cobwebs	horizontal

1. the act of forming circles ☐ ☐ ☐ ☐ ☐ ☐ ☐ ☐
   1 11

2. straight up and down ☐ ☐ ☐ ☐ ☐ ☐ ☐ ☐
   3

3. bends easily ☐ ☐ ☐ ☐ ☐ ☐ ☐ ☐
   10   6

4. shapes with two long sides, two short sides, and right angles

   ☐ ☐ ☐ ☐ ☐ ☐ ☐ ☐ ☐ ☐
   12

5. webs made by some spiders ☐ ☐ ☐ ☐ ☐ ☐ ☐
   4

6. in the same direction as the horizon

   ☐ ☐ ☐ ☐ ☐ ☐ ☐ ☐ ☐ ☐
   5

7. hangs down while attached to something

   ☐ ☐ ☐ ☐ ☐ ☐ ☐ ☐
   7   13

8. can be destroyed easily ☐ ☐ ☐ ☐ ☐ ☐ ☐
   9   2 8

ANSWER:

☐ ☐ ☐ ☐ ☐ ☐ ☐ ☐   ☐ ☐ ☐ ☐ ☐ !
1 2 3 4 5 6 7 8   9 10 11 12 13

Directions: Read the phrase. Look for the word or words that have the same or almost the same meaning as the boldfaced word. Mark the answer space for your choice.

 Tip Always read all the answer choices. Many choices may make sense. But only one answer choice has the same or almost the same meaning as the **boldfaced** word.

1. **suspends** a hammock
   Ⓐ separates
   Ⓑ hangs
   Ⓒ extends
   Ⓓ fixes

2. **encircles** the word
   Ⓕ puts a circle around
   Ⓖ takes a circle away
   Ⓗ earns
   Ⓙ repeats

3. **flexible** rim
   Ⓐ fallen
   Ⓑ attaches easily
   Ⓒ bends easily
   Ⓓ expected

4. **circular** driveway
   Ⓕ in a flat shape
   Ⓖ in a car's shape
   Ⓗ deep and long
   Ⓙ in a circle shape

5. **fragile** vase
   Ⓐ frightened
   Ⓑ delicate
   Ⓒ enormous
   Ⓓ new

6. old **cobwebs**
   Ⓕ spider webs
   Ⓖ puzzles
   Ⓗ corn cobs
   Ⓙ barns

7. **horizontal** line
   Ⓐ curved
   Ⓑ like the horizon
   Ⓒ black
   Ⓓ around the earth

8. **vertical** pole
   Ⓕ up and down
   Ⓖ back and forth
   Ⓗ long
   Ⓙ valuable

9. measure the **diameter**
   Ⓐ area of room
   Ⓑ ingredients
   Ⓒ line around a square
   Ⓓ line through a circle

10. wood **rectangles**
    Ⓕ shapes with four sides
    Ⓖ apartments
    Ⓗ shapes with three sides
    Ⓙ sculptures

Review

1. **poisonous** snake
   Ⓐ harmful
   Ⓑ colorful
   Ⓒ long
   Ⓓ pointing

2. **conceal** the ball
   Ⓕ roll
   Ⓖ reveal
   Ⓗ share
   Ⓙ hide

3. **attentive** students
   Ⓐ lazy
   Ⓑ sleepy
   Ⓒ alert
   Ⓓ quick

4. **devour** apples
   Ⓕ devote
   Ⓖ eat
   Ⓗ bake
   Ⓙ collect

5. simple **procedure**
   Ⓐ parade
   Ⓑ procession
   Ⓒ method
   Ⓓ excuse

Writing

Spiders are not the only creatures that build their own homes. Bees build hives and birds build nests. Men and women also build houses. Each home fits the needs of the person or animal that lives in it.

Compare a spider's home with one of these other homes. Explain how they are alike and how they are different. Think about the shapes of the homes and the building materials used to create them. Also think about the purpose for each home. Use the pictures and information from the story to help you. Use some vocabulary words in your writing.

_____

_____

_____

_____

_____

_____

_____

_____

_____

_____

_____

_____

_____

_____

Turn to "My Personal Word List" on page 132. Write some words from the story or other words that you would like to know more about. Use a dictionary to find the meanings.

★ To review the words in Lessons 13–16, turn to page 128. ★

REMARKABLE ROBOTS

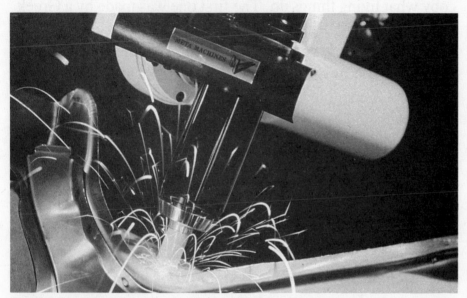

A robot never tires. It can work without stopping. A few drops of oil are all it may need to keep going. Many robots are found in factories. Some even star in movies!

In Lessons 17–20, you will learn about some robots. Think about robots you've seen in the movies or on television. How did they look? How did they sound? What jobs did they perform? Write your words on the lines below.

How Robots Look and Sound	Jobs Robots Can Do
_____	_____
_____	_____
_____	_____
_____	_____
_____	_____

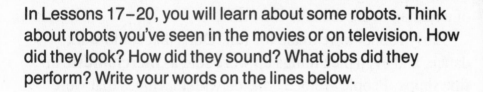

★ Read the story below. Think about the meanings of
the **boldfaced** words. ★

How Robots Came to Be

Robots seem very new to most people. But they have a long
history. They began as mechanical toys. For more than two
thousand years, people have been trying to make machines that
copy what living things do. The first one was made by a Greek
inventor. He built a pigeon that looked real, though it was
artificial. The bird could **rotate**, turning on the end of a
wooden bar. A **device** like this sounds simple to us. But the
strange bird delighted the Greeks of long ago.

Workers in France built a mechanical lion in 1500. To get it
to work, they **rebuilt** the lion several times. Finally, it was able
to walk around the court of the king. It could even raise its paw
as a salute to the French flag.

In the 1700s, a Swiss clockmaker built a puppet. The
puppet's right hand was **equipped** with a pen. The clockmaker
would hook a machine to his own arm and write a message.
The machine inside the puppet would copy his arm
movements. The puppet was able to write the same message as
the clockmaker. The puppet seemed to have the **intelligence** of
a thinking being. However, it needed the **assistance**, or help,
of a human being to make it work.

Early robots were made for fun. Dolls that could walk,
dance, and even pick things up were sold as **merchandise** in
fine shops. People seemed amazed with machines that were
automatic. They could operate by themselves once they had
been turned on.

Today's robots are very complicated machines with many
different uses. They work in modern factories. They help to
build automobiles, watches, and plastic food containers.
Robots are exploring the oceans and working in space. The
uses of robots seem endless.

★ Go back to the story. Underline the words or sentences that give
you a clue to the meaning of each **boldfaced** word. ★

CONTEXT CLUES

Read each sentence below. Choose a word from the box that means the same as the underlined part of each sentence. Write the word on the line after the sentence.

rebuilt	automatic	robots	rotate
artificial	merchandise	device	intelligence
equipped	assistance		

1. Today, <u>machines that perform some activities of a human being</u> have many uses. _____

2. The controls on an airplane that are <u>able to work by themselves</u> help a pilot keep the plane on course. _____

3. The pilot of an airplane appreciates this <u>help</u>. _____

4. This type of <u>machine</u> became popular long ago. _____

5. A German inventor once built a <u>fake</u> eagle that could fly. _____

6. Although the inventor <u>fitted</u> the eagle with wings, it could not fly gracefully. _____

7. On some old clocks, carved figures <u>move around in a circle</u>. _____

8. One of these clocks, built in 1352, was later <u>built again</u> in the sixteenth century. _____

9. Who knows what future uses the human <u>mind</u> will find for these kinds of machines? _____

10. This kind of <u>product</u> may someday be found in stores to help us with many human tasks. _____

CLASSIFYING

Write each word from the box in the group where it belongs.

| device | merchandise | automatic |
| robots | artificial | |

HUMAN-LIKE MACHINES

Names for These Machines

1. _____

2. _____

3. _____

Qualities of These Machines

4. _____

5. _____

DICTIONARY SKILLS

Read each question. For a "yes" answer, write <u>yes</u> on the line. For a "no" answer, write a sentence that gives the correct meaning of the underlined word. Use the Dictionary if you need help.

1. Is a fully <u>equipped</u> gym empty?

_____

2. If a planet <u>rotates</u>, does it bounce?

_____

3. Is a brand-new car <u>rebuilt</u>?

_____

4. Does an <u>automatic</u> machine perform a task by itself?

_____

5. If you give <u>assistance</u> to people, are you ignoring them?

_____

6. If you are using your <u>intelligence</u>, are you using your ability to learn and understand?

_____

CROSSWORD PUZZLE

Use the clues and the words in the box to complete the crossword puzzle.

rebuilt	automatic	robots	rotate
artificial	merchandise	device	intelligence
equipped	assistance		

Across
1. help or aid
5. machines that imitate humans
7. machine
8. products; goods

Down
1. not real
2. ability to know
3. acting or moving by itself
4. provided with all that is needed
5. built again
6. to make a circle around from one point

 GET WISE TO TESTS

Directions: Read each sentence. Pick the word that best completes the sentence. Mark the letter for that word.

Read carefully. Use the other words in the sentence to help you choose the missing word.

1. Myra _____ the engine with parts from other old engines.
   - Ⓐ her
   - Ⓒ rebuilt
   - Ⓑ profit
   - Ⓓ artificial

2. The factory used _____ to do work too dangerous for people.
   - Ⓕ automatic
   - Ⓗ qualify
   - Ⓖ robots
   - Ⓙ diary

3. The shop was _____ with every tool you could imagine.
   - Ⓐ equipped
   - Ⓒ read
   - Ⓑ fluid
   - Ⓓ merchandise

4. The _____ used to lift heavy stone was interesting to watch.
   - Ⓕ rebuilt
   - Ⓗ drawn
   - Ⓖ physical
   - Ⓙ device

5. They made a carrot that could not be eaten because it was _____.
   - Ⓐ artificial
   - Ⓒ automatic
   - Ⓑ rinse
   - Ⓓ machine

6. Earth and other planets _____ around the sun.
   - Ⓕ speak
   - Ⓗ rotate
   - Ⓖ robots
   - Ⓙ device

7. The students gave their _____ to help complete the mural.
   - Ⓐ rotate
   - Ⓒ corridor
   - Ⓑ assistance
   - Ⓓ sneaks

8. The store had all kinds of interesting _____.
   - Ⓕ breeze
   - Ⓗ rebuilt
   - Ⓖ associate
   - Ⓙ merchandise

9. You do not have to turn the crank because this machine is _____.
   - Ⓐ device
   - Ⓒ automatic
   - Ⓑ earnest
   - Ⓓ merchandise

10. A person who speaks well shows _____.
    - Ⓕ intelligence
    - Ⓗ robots
    - Ⓖ painful
    - Ⓙ easily

Writing

Imagine that you are at a party with your friends. Suddenly, to everyone's surprise, you become a robot. What about you stays the same when you become a robot? What about you changes when you are a robot?

   Write a paragraph that describes the scene at the party after this amazing change. Compare your appearance and actions before and after the change. The picture on this page might help you with ideas. Use some vocabulary words in your writing.

   Suddenly, to everyone's surprise at the party, I changed

into _____

_____

_____

_____

_____

_____

_____

_____

_____

_____

_____

_____

_____

_____

Turn to "My Personal Word List" on page 132. Write some words from the story or other words that you would like to know more about. Use a dictionary to find the meanings.

★ Read the children's story below. Think about the meanings of the **boldfaced** words. ★

My Robot Buddy

Jack Jameson wanted a robot for his birthday more than anything in the world. At last his parents said yes!

On Saturday, Mom, Dad, and I drove in Dad's **solar** car to Metropolis VII. Dad drove up one ramp and then another, and in a few moments we saw a big sign that said:

ATKINS ROBOTS, INC.
THE VERY BEST IN ROBOTS

Behind the sign was a circular white building. We drove up the ramp right into the building and came to a sign that blinked:

STOP
LEAVE YOUR MOTOR ON
NOW LEAVE THE CAR

"It looks pretty efficient," Dad said.

We all turned. Standing there was a tall, thin man wearing a green **smock** and carrying a **clipboard** with papers on it.

"I am Dr. Atkins. And you, I take it, are the Jameson family. If you will please follow me, we will begin our tour of the factory."

We followed Dr. Atkins into a small room in which were three chairs facing a blank white wall.

"Please sit down."

He pushed a button. It was completely dark in the room now. The wall now seemed to be melting in front of our very eyes. We were looking right through it into a long room. In the middle of the room was a **conveyor belt** with robots lying down on it. Standing above them, working on them, wiring them, soldering **connections**, attaching terminals, were other robots. Robots were manufacturing other robots!

"In **PRODUCTION**," Dr. Atkin's voice rang out, "we construct the outer shells and the inner hardware. We are now coming to our second *P* department — PROGRAMMING."

Seated at a row of machines with **keyboards** were a dozen older people punching out computer data cards.

PROGRAMMING disappeared. The factory appeared to glide along behind the wall again.

"Now we are coming to PHYSIOGNOMY– which means, young man?"

"Faces," I said.

"Very good. What kind of face would you like your robot to have?"

"Can I see some?" I asked.

I saw more than some. There were boy faces and girl faces. Faces with pug noses, long noses, big ears, little ears, buckteeth, little teeth, no teeth; redheads, blonds, dark-haired kids.

"Do you see any face you like, Jack?" Mom asked.

"Lots," I said. "Hey, there's a swell face."

It was a boy who looked about my age. He had red hair and freckles. He was grinning. It was a friendly face.

"We are now arriving at our **PERSONALITY** department." We were looking into another room. This one had a **gigantic** computer in it.

"Young man, if you were to have a robot for a friend, what kind of personality would you like him to have?"

"Well," I said, looking at the computer where a single light was going on and off. "I like outdoor things. I like baseball and football and I like to fish. I'm a good tree climber and a pretty fast runner."

Suddenly there was a knock on the door.

"Come in," Dr. Atkins said.

The door opened. A red-headed kid with freckles was standing there. He had a paper in his hand.

"Happy birthday, Jack," the kid said, grinning. "Here's my **printout**, Dr. Atkins. I hope he likes me."

Danny One and I stood there grinning at each other.

This was both our birthdays.

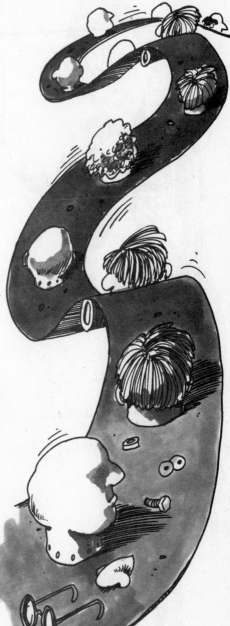

From My Robot Buddy, by
Alfred Slote

★ Go back to the story. Underline any words or sentences that give you clues to the meanings of the **boldfaced** words. ★

CONTEXT CLUES

Read each pair of sentences. Look for a clue in the first sentence to help you choose the missing word in the second sentence. Write the word from the box that completes each sentence.

keyboards	clipboard	smock	production
printout	personality	solar	connections
gigantic	conveyor belt		

1. Jack's family rode to the robot factory in a car that was powered by the sun. It ran on _____ energy.

2. The factory was very large. Later, Jack described it to his friends as being _____.

3. A man wearing a big shirt that protected his clothing from dirt greeted them. His name was on his _____.

4. The man carried a paper holder that had a big clip at the top. He checked his _____ to find Jack's name.

5. Inside the factory, Jack saw robots being moved from one place to the next. They were on a _____.

6. Jack and his parents were in a part of the factory where the robots were made. It was the _____ area.

7. Robots were joining parts of other robots together. They were careful to be sure the _____ would hold.

8. People working at computers typed in the number of robots made. They were typing on _____.

9. Danny One carried a sheet of paper that had come from a computer. The _____ told all about him.

10. Jack wanted Danny One to like the same things that he did. He got a robot with a _____ like his own.

WORD GROUPS

Read each pair of words. Think about how they are alike. Write the word from the box that best completes each group.

gigantic	clipboard	smock
keyboard	conveyor belt	connections

1. notebook, folder, _____

2. glove, apron, _____

3. printer, screen, _____

4. links, joints, _____

5. huge, monstrous, _____

6. transporter, carrier, _____

DICTIONARY SKILLS

Each numbered example has two parts. Answer the first part by writing a word from the box. Answer the second part by circling the correct choice. Use the **pronunciation key** on page 133 to help you when necessary.

production	solar	printout	personality

1. Write the spelling of sō′lər. _____

   It means **a.** produced by the sun **b.** produced by soldiers

2. Write the spelling of prə duk′ shən. _____

   It means **a.** the act of making **b.** the act of selling

3. Write the spelling of pûr′sə nal′i tē. _____

   It means **a.** what a person looks like **b.** what a person is like

4. Write the spelling of print′out′. _____

   It means **a.** notebook paper **b.** computer paper

GET WISE TO TESTS

Directions: Read each sentence. Pick the word that best completes the sentence. Mark the answer space for that word.

 Before you choose an answer, try reading the sentence with each answer choice. This will help you choose an answer that makes sense.

1. Televisions were assembled on the _____.
   Ⓐ clipboard
   Ⓑ conveyor belt
   Ⓒ watching
   Ⓓ spray

2. A _____ was made of the computer drawing.
   Ⓕ printout
   Ⓖ typing
   Ⓗ quickly
   Ⓙ keyboard

3. Wear this _____ over your new outfit.
   Ⓐ smock
   Ⓑ ring
   Ⓒ driving
   Ⓓ conveyor belt

4. How many trucks are in _____ now?
   Ⓕ wastes
   Ⓖ culture
   Ⓗ production
   Ⓙ smock

5. These important _____ allow a machine to work.
   Ⓐ personality
   Ⓑ connections
   Ⓒ admire
   Ⓓ buttoned

6. All computers have _____ for entering the commands.
   Ⓕ clipboards
   Ⓖ person
   Ⓗ aloft
   Ⓙ keyboards

7. _____ panels on top of the house collected the sun's energy.
   Ⓐ Because
   Ⓑ Connection
   Ⓒ Solar
   Ⓓ Cooler

8. Her _____ made her popular with many people.
   Ⓕ personality
   Ⓖ sideways
   Ⓗ keyboards
   Ⓙ smiled

9. The _____ elephant could not fit into the cage.
   Ⓐ hesitate
   Ⓑ solar
   Ⓒ tiny
   Ⓓ gigantic

10. The coach had a paper on her _____ with notes about the game.
    Ⓕ dressing
    Ⓖ endless
    Ⓗ clipboard
    Ⓙ equipment

Review

1. I could tell those plastic flowers were _____.
   Ⓐ bloom
   Ⓑ dead
   Ⓒ artificial
   Ⓓ smelling

2. The kind people at the information booth gave us some _____.
   Ⓕ way
   Ⓖ helping
   Ⓗ roads
   Ⓙ assistance

Writing

Think ahead to a future time. Imagine that you are on your way to a robot factory to order your own Danny One.

On the lines below, describe your robot. Explain what it will look like. Also describe the kind of personality you want your robot to have. Finally, explain why you are getting a robot and what you plan to do with it. Use some vocabulary words in your writing.

_____

_____

_____

_____

_____

_____

_____

_____

_____

_____

_____

_____

_____

_____

_____

_____

_____

_____

_____

Turn to "My Personal Word List" on page 132. Write some words from the story or other words that you would like to know more about. Use a dictionary to find the meanings.

★ Read the story below. Think about the meanings of the **boldfaced** words. ★

What a Worker!

Imagine a worker who never gets tired. This **employee** needs no lunch hours or holidays. Working 24 hours a day is no problem. Best of all, he or she is both **accurate** and **efficient**. There are few mistakes and tasks are finished quickly.

Any **manufacturer** would want a worker like this in a factory. Many more products could be made and sold if workers never stopped. That's why there are more and more robots at work today.

Robots do a wide **variety** of tasks. They weld, drill, and paint new cars. They locate underwater pollution sites. Robots handle poisons. Most of their work is too dangerous, difficult, or unpleasant for people to do. By doing the dirty work, a robot is a worker's helper, or **aide**.

Few robots look anything like people. They are machines. Like other pieces of **machinery**, they come in different shapes and sizes. The way they are built depends on the jobs they do. Most have a single arm that can lift things. Most are built to handle tools.

Each robot has a computer inside it. The computer tells it what to do. Skilled **technicians** enter directions into this computer. They are trained for this job.

The years ahead may well be the **era** of robots. People are using them more and more. Already robots have explored active volcanoes and the ocean floor. Modern robots can **maneuver** in space. With their skillful movements, they can service satellites that cannot be reached by humans. Some new uses will include harvesting crops and working in open pit mines. Robots can help us to live better and learn more about our world.

★ Go back to the story. Underline the words or sentences that give you a clue to the meaning of each **boldfaced** word. ★

CONTEXT CLUES

Read each pair of sentences. Look for a clue in the first sentence to help you choose the missing word in the second sentence. Write the word from the box that best completes the sentence.

technician	accurate	efficient	machinery
manufacturer	era	variety	employee
maneuver	aide		

1. Some robots seem to be able to think. They appear to be human beings, rather than pieces of _____.

2. When a robot needs repair, a trained person must fix it. Only a _____ can do this job.

3. Robots help human workers by making and packing articles. They can do a wide _____ of jobs.

4. Some workers wonder if robots are a help. A robot is not an _____ if it does a job poorly.

5. Sometimes the head of a factory will replace a human worker with a robot. The _____ wants to get the job done in the best possible way.

6. In most cases, the human worker moves on to another task. The _____ can do work that a robot can't.

7. A mechanical lion was made in the 1500s. There were many inventions during this _____.

8. Moving robots can sense something in their path. They _____ away from it.

9. A robot does its work without wasting time or energy. It is an _____ servant.

10. Computers must give robots correct instructions. Humans make the instructions _____.

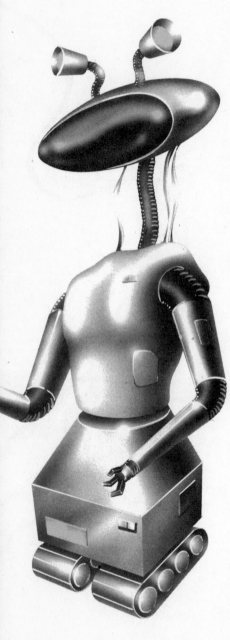

WORD SENSE

Read each phrase. Check the Dictionary to see if the words make sense together. If they do, write <u>yes</u> on the line. If they do not, think of a word that does make sense with the underlined word. Write your word and the underlined word on the line.

accurate	employee	manufacturer	aide	machinery

1. leaf <u>manufacturer</u> _____

2. <u>employee</u> union _____

3. silly <u>machinery</u> _____

4. <u>accurate</u> tree _____

5. doll's <u>aide</u> _____

CLOZE PARAGRAPH

Use the words in the box to complete the paragraph. Reread the paragraph to be sure it makes sense.

variety	technicians	efficient
maneuver	employee	era

In some ways, the twentieth century seems to be the

(1) _____ of the robot. Few people are

surprised to see a robot as an (2) _____. Skilled

(3) _____ have designed robots to perform all
sorts of tasks that humans might find boring. The robots can

(4) _____ quickly. They do dull work in an

(5) _____ way. Human workers can move on to

a (6) _____ of more interesting jobs.

GET WISE TO TESTS

Directions: Read the phrase. Look for the word or words that have the same or almost the same meaning as the boldfaced word. Mark the answer space for your choice.

 Think about the meanings of the **boldfaced** word. Don't be fooled by a word that looks similar to it.

1. **maneuver** carefully
   Ⓐ speak
   Ⓑ manage
   Ⓒ move
   Ⓓ think

2. teacher's **aide**
   Ⓕ aim
   Ⓖ helper
   Ⓗ advice
   Ⓙ vacation

3. **accurate** answers
   Ⓐ correct
   Ⓑ assured
   Ⓒ sloppy
   Ⓓ neat

4. important **era**
   Ⓕ mistake
   Ⓖ period of time
   Ⓗ group of errors
   Ⓙ way of life

5. modern **machinery**
   Ⓐ marchers
   Ⓑ style
   Ⓒ equipment
   Ⓓ magazines

6. tool **manufacturer**
   Ⓕ maker
   Ⓖ buyer
   Ⓗ musician
   Ⓙ borrower

7. medical **technician**
   Ⓐ patient
   Ⓑ expert
   Ⓒ doctor
   Ⓓ teammate

8. **efficient** use
   Ⓕ poor
   Ⓖ good
   Ⓗ cheerful
   Ⓙ effected

9. wide **variety**
   Ⓐ mixture
   Ⓑ structure
   Ⓒ valley
   Ⓓ cargo

10. paid **employee**
    Ⓕ empire
    Ⓖ worker
    Ⓗ observer
    Ⓙ occasion

Review

1. **artificial** flavor
   Ⓐ article
   Ⓑ fake
   Ⓒ real
   Ⓓ splendid

2. new **device**
   Ⓕ invention
   Ⓖ advice
   Ⓗ diver
   Ⓙ food

3. **assistance** needed
   Ⓐ assignment
   Ⓑ silence
   Ⓒ help
   Ⓓ loneliness

4. fine **merchandise**
   Ⓕ friendship
   Ⓖ method
   Ⓗ merchants
   Ⓙ goods

5. **precise** amount
   Ⓐ exact
   Ⓑ precious
   Ⓒ percent
   Ⓓ unsure

Writing

Pretend that the people who live in your city are about to vote on whether or not they want robots in school. Do you think a robot could improve your school? How might a robot help the students and teachers? If you had to vote for robots in your school would you vote yes or no?

Write a speech you might give to persuade others to vote yes or no for robots in the classroom. Remember to include reasons and examples to convince your listeners. Use some vocabulary words in your writing.

Do I want robots in the classroom? My vote is _____

_____

_____

_____

_____

_____

_____

_____

_____

_____

_____

_____

_____

_____

_____

Turn to "My Personal Word List" on page 132. Write some words from the story or other words that you would like to know more about. Use a dictionary to find the meanings.

★ Read the story below. Think about the meanings of the **boldfaced** words. ★

Real Art?

For many years, people have written stories about robots. Sometimes these robots are strange beings from other planets in our solar system. Sometimes they come from other **galaxies**. Many Earth beings in the stories are eager to meet these **alien** beings from far away.

Sometimes the robots in stories are good. Sometimes they are not. Some story robots are clever **villains** who have fought to take over the world with their evil powers. They have **clashed** with the humans.

Almost every movie **version** of a robot story has been well liked by people who watch movies. To many movie **viewers**, the robots in the 1977 movie *Star Wars* are the real stars of the show. These good robots, C3PO and R2D2, are **dependable**. They can be trusted. They are also eager to help the humans. They are not **ambitious** for power.

Make-believe robots are interesting. Today, though, they cannot hold more **fascination** than real robots. For example, one real robot is an artist. Meet Aaron, a robot who paints pictures of people.

Aaron is not a simple robot. He is an **elaborate** computer system developed over the last 25 years by artist Harold Cohen. Cohen wrote computer software to teach Aaron to paint. Aaron learned about drawing and painting and about the world. After many years of training, Aaron now paints shapes and faces. His paintings can be seen in museums around the world. They are more popular than Cohen's own paintings.

For a long time, Aaron painted what Cohen told him to paint. Now Cohen says that Aaron decides what to paint. Can paintings created by a robot be real art? What do you think?

★ Go back to the story. Underline the words or sentences that give you a clue to the meaning of each **boldfaced** word. ★

USING CONTEXT

Meanings for the vocabulary words are given below. Go back to the story and read each sentence that has a vocabulary word. If you still cannot tell the meaning, look for clues in the sentences that come before and after the one with the vocabulary word. Write each word in front of its meaning.

dependable	villains	alien	ambitious
fascination	version	clashed	viewers
elaborate	galaxies		

1. _____ : people who look at or watch something

2. _____ : a special form

3. _____ : trustworthy

4. _____ : had a conflict; fought

5. _____ : from another planet; foreign

6. _____ : a strong interest or attraction

7. _____ : evil creatures

8. _____ : seeking something better

9. _____ : complicated

10. _____ : large groups of stars

CHALLENGE YOURSELF

Name two places where you would find <u>viewers</u>.

_____   _____

Name two characters in books or movies who are <u>villains</u>.

_____   _____

ANTONYMS

Remember that **antonyms** are words that have opposite meanings. Write a word from the box that is an antonym for the underlined word or words in each sentence.

elaborate	ambitious	alien
dependable	fascination	

1. She started with a <u>simple</u> plan that soon became very

    _____ .

2. My cousin has a great _____ with mystery stories. For me, they bring on <u>boredom</u>.

3. She is _____ , but her younger sister is <u>unreliable</u>.

4. Is the new worker _____ , or is he <u>lazy</u> and <u>uncaring</u>?

5. The strange creature was certainly not a <u>native</u>; it was an

    _____ .

REWRITING SENTENCES

Rewrite each sentence using a vocabulary word from the box.

dependable	villains	version	galaxies

1. I have always wanted to visit other groups of stars.

    _____

2. I would take along my trustworthy robot.

    _____

3. We would fight and conquer many evil creatures.

    _____

4. I could write a book, and it could be made into a movie form.

    _____

121

RELATED WORDS

Read each sentence. Find a word that is related to one of the words in the box. Underline the word in the sentence. Then write the word from the box on the line.

fascination	viewers	ambitious
dependable	elaborate	

1. Art lovers are fascinated by the idea that paintings can be done by a robot. _____

2. Many people have gone to museums to view Aaron's paintings. _____

3. Aaron runs on an elaborately designed computer program.

   _____

4. Aaron's ability to paint depends on the computer program.

   _____

5. Harold Cohen has achieved his ambition to create a robot artist. _____

WORD SENSE

Read each phrase. Check the Dictionary to see if the words make sense together. If they do, write yes on the line. If they do not, think of a word that does make sense with the underlined word. Write your word and the underlined word on the line.

1. distant <u>galaxies</u> _____

2. kind <u>villains</u> _____

3. ambitious <u>slippers</u> _____

4. constant <u>fascination</u> _____

5. alien <u>natives</u> _____

6. numerous <u>viewers</u> _____

7. dependable <u>nostrils</u> _____

Directions: Read the sentences. Look for the best word to use in the blank. Mark the answer space for your choice.

Tip If you are not sure which word completes the sentence, do the best you can. Try to choose the answer that makes the most sense.

1. That is one of the most popular programs on TV. It has millions of _____.
   - Ⓐ trainers
   - Ⓒ writers
   - Ⓑ viewers
   - Ⓓ galaxies

2. Carol always arrives on time. She is very _____.
   - Ⓕ expensive
   - Ⓗ costly
   - Ⓖ elaborate
   - Ⓙ dependable

3. For months the thieves robbed stores. Finally, the police caught the _____.
   - Ⓐ viewers
   - Ⓒ galaxies
   - Ⓑ villains
   - Ⓓ gestures

4. He claimed that a spaceship landed. Out of the craft came _____ visitors.
   - Ⓕ alien
   - Ⓗ loud
   - Ⓖ diamond
   - Ⓙ furniture

5. The two enemies could never agree about anything. They always _____.
   - Ⓐ clashed
   - Ⓒ agreed
   - Ⓑ helped
   - Ⓓ elaborated

6. Look at the stars through this telescope. You will be able to see far-off _____.
   - Ⓕ buildings
   - Ⓗ galaxies
   - Ⓖ mountains
   - Ⓙ fascination

7. The cat could not take its eyes off the canaries. It stared at them with _____.
   - Ⓐ fascination
   - Ⓒ disgust
   - Ⓑ glasses
   - Ⓓ swarms

8. The necklace had beads of many different colors and shapes. The design was very _____.
   - Ⓕ dependable
   - Ⓗ stem
   - Ⓖ plain
   - Ⓙ elaborate

9. I saw both the play and the film. I preferred the film _____.
   - Ⓐ fascination
   - Ⓒ version
   - Ⓑ light
   - Ⓓ boundary

10. Her goal was to make important discoveries in science. She was very _____.
    - Ⓕ tired
    - Ⓗ clashed
    - Ⓖ ambitious
    - Ⓙ dependable

Review

1. She rarely made mistakes. Her work was very _____.
   - Ⓐ messy
   - Ⓒ accurate
   - Ⓑ sloppy
   - Ⓓ unhappy

2. He needed help to finish the job. A robot would be his _____.
   - Ⓕ aide
   - Ⓗ lunch
   - Ⓖ enemy
   - Ⓙ problem

Robots have been taught to help build cars, assemble watches, and assist doctors. Think of some new tasks that robots could learn to help people. Use your imagination!

On the lines below, tell about three jobs that robots could do for you. Tell why robots would be good for these jobs. Use some vocabulary words in your writing.

_____

_____

_____

_____

_____

_____

_____

_____

_____

_____

_____

_____

_____

_____

_____

_____

_____

_____

_____

Turn to "My Personal Word List" on page 132. Write some words from the story or other words that you would like to know more about. Use a dictionary to find the meanings.

★ To review the words in Lessons 17–20, turn to page 129. ★

Read each clue. Then write the word from the box that fits the clue. Use the Dictionary if you need help.

historic	glimmer	pyramids	investigate
debris	spiny	navigate	sunken
buoy	jewelry		

1. If you went to see the tomb of King Tutankhamen in Egypt, you would see these. _____

2. Rubies and emeralds are often used to create this.

   _____

3. A sea creature with long spines could be called this.

   _____

4. When people try to solve a mystery, they often do this.

   _____

5. If you see a floating signal in the water, you may have found this. _____

6. When a very important world event happens, we say it is this. _____

7. If you want to go to sea in a sailboat, you need to know how to do this. _____

8. When gems and crystals shine, they do this.

   _____

9. After a treasure chest has dropped to the bottom of the sea, we say it is this. _____

10. After a tornado has passed, you would probably find this.

    _____

Read each question. Think about the meaning of the underlined word. Then write yes or no to answer the question. Use the Dictionary if you need help.

1. Would a shark prey on other fish? _____

2. Would most people enjoy being held captive? _____

3. If an airplane pilot wants to know what time it is, should she check her altitude? _____

4. If you need a ride to work, do you need to get a sensation? _____

5. Is an airplane airborne after it leaves the ground? _____

6. Would you find mortals at a football game? _____

7. If you read every day, are you dedicated to learning? _____

8. Do birds and fish belong to the same species? _____

9. If you like to stay up late at night, do you like to hibernate? _____

10. If people recommend a restaurant, do they probably enjoy eating there? _____

11. If you want a clear answer to a question, do you want the person to respond vaguely? _____

12. If you were flying in a plane, would you have an aerial view of the earth? _____

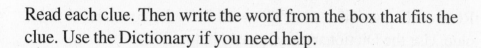

Read each clue. Then write the word from the box that fits the clue. Use the Dictionary if you need help.

injured	strengthen	maintain	long-term
prejudice	alternate	superb	popularity
sequence	positive		

1. To keep from losing your math skills, you must do this to them. _____

2. If you dislike a group of people for no reason, you show this. _____

3. If you think your lunch is excellent, you might use this word to describe it. _____

4. When you put words in alphabetical order, you put them in this. _____

5. If the muscles in your arms are weak, you need to do this to them. _____

6. If you break your leg, you could be called this.

   _____

7. When you are very sure of something, you could be described as this. _____

8. If you plan to spend years in school and become a lawyer, you have this kind of goal. _____

9. If you played in a game because another team member got hurt, you would be this. _____

10. When you are liked by everyone, you have this.

    _____

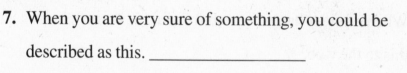

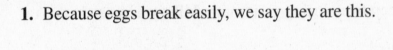

Read each clue. Then write the word from the box that fits the clue. Use the Dictionary if you need help.

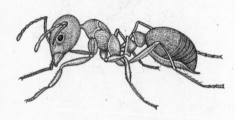

vertical	authority	caravan	fragile
defend	grit	attentive	suspends
haven	conceal		

1. Because eggs break easily, we say they are this.

   _____

2. If you do not want anyone to find you, you might do this to yourself. _____

3. If you are in the woods when a blizzard comes, you might call a warm cabin this. _____

4. When lines go up and down, they are this.

   _____

5. If you spend all day at the beach, this is what you will find in your clothes. _____

6. When you are in charge of a situation, you have this.

   _____

7. When a spider hangs its web from a tree branch, it does this to the web. _____

8. You are this when you are paying close attention to what someone says. _____

9. When mother lions keep other animals away from their cubs, they do this. _____

10. If a group of cars travel together, they could be called this.

   _____

REVIEW

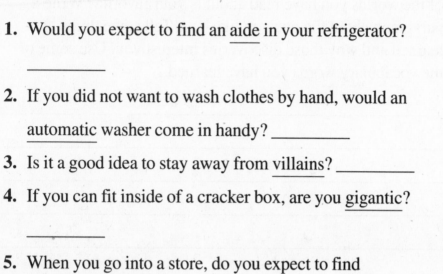

Read each question. Think about the meaning of the underlined word. Then write yes or no to answer the question. Use the Dictionary if you need help.

1. Would you expect to find an aide in your refrigerator?

   _____

2. If you did not want to wash clothes by hand, would an automatic washer come in handy? _____

3. Is it a good idea to stay away from villains? _____

4. If you can fit inside of a cracker box, are you gigantic?

   _____

5. When you go into a store, do you expect to find merchandise there? _____

6. If two people clashed, did they agree on everything?

   _____

7. When a puppy chases its tail, does it rotate? _____

8. If you have a fascination with dolphins, do you probably want to learn more about them? _____

9. Would you be able to maneuver a bicycle that had no handlebars? _____

10. Does your brain use solar power? _____

11. If you have a smock, should you see a doctor? _____

12. Would working quickly and carefully be efficient?

   _____

REVIEW AND WRITE

In this book, you have explored many different worlds. For example, you have learned about the world of buried treasure, the worlds of small creatures, and the world of robots. Which of the worlds you have read about is your favorite? Write a paragraph about the one you like best. Tell some things you learned and why those discoveries interest you. Use some of the vocabulary words you have learned.

_____

_____

_____

_____

_____

_____

_____

_____

_____

_____

_____

_____

_____

_____

_____

_____

_____

_____

_____

_____

_____

MY PERSONAL WORD LIST

This is your word list. Here you can write words from the stories. You can also write other words that you would like to know more about. Use a dictionary to find the meaning of each word. Then write the meaning next to the word.

UNIT 1
BURIED TREASURE

_____

_____

_____

_____

_____

_____

_____

UNIT 2
UP, UP, AND AWAY

_____

_____

_____

_____

_____

_____

My Personal Word List

UNIT 3
SPORTS WATCH

_____

_____

_____

_____

_____

UNIT 4
SMALL WORLDS

_____

_____

_____

_____

_____

UNIT 5
REMARKABLE ROBOTS

_____

_____

_____

_____

_____

_____

DICTIONARY

ENTRY

Each word in a dictionary is called an **entry word**. Study the parts of an entry in the sample shown below. Think about how each part will help you when you read and write.

① **Entry Word** An entry word is boldfaced. A dot is used to divide the word into syllables.

② **Pronunciation** This special spelling shows you how to say the word. Look at the pronunciation key below. It tells you the symbols that stand for sounds.

③ **Part of Speech** The abbreviation tells you the part of speech. In this entry *v.* stands for verb.

④ **Words with Spelling Changes** When the spelling of a word changes after *-ed* and *-ing* are added, it is shown in an entry.

⑤ **Definition** A definition is given for each entry word. The definition tells what the word means.

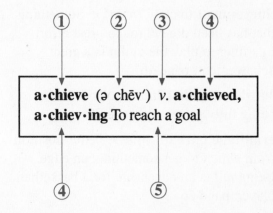

PRONUNCIATION KEY

A **pronunciation key** is a helpful tool. It shows you the symbols, or special signs, for the sounds in English. Next to each symbol is a sample word for that sound. Use the key to help you with the pronunciation given after each entry word.

a	at, bad		d	dear, soda, bad
ā	ape, pain, day, break		f	five, defend, leaf, off, cough, elephant
ä	father, car, heart		g	game, ago, fog, egg
âr	care, pair, bear, their, where		h	hat, ahead
e	end, pet, said, heaven, friend		hw	white, whether, which
ē	equal, me, feet, team, piece, key		j	joke, enjoy, gem, page, edge
i	it, big, English, hymn		k	kite, bakery, seek, tack, cat
ī	ice, fine, lie, my		l	lid, sailor, feel, ball, allow
îr	ear, deer, here, pierce		m	man, family, dream
o	odd, hot, watch		n	not, final, pan, knife
ō	old, oat, toe, low		ng	long, singer, pink
ô	coffee, all, taught, law, fought		p	pail, repair, soap, happy
ôr	order, fork, horse, story, pour		r	ride, parent, wear, more, marry
oi	oil, toy		s	sit, aside, pets, cent, pass
ou	out, now		sh	shoe, washer, fish, mission, nation
u	up, mud, love, double		t	tag, pretend, fat, button, dressed
ū	use, mule, cue, feud, few		th	thin, panther, both
ü	rule, true, food		<u>th</u>	this, mother, smooth
u̇	put, wood, should		v	very, favor, wave
ûr	burn, hurry, term, bird, word, courage		w	wet, weather, reward
ə	about, taken, pencil, lemon, circus		y	yes, onion
b	bat, above, job		z	zoo, lazy, jazz, rose, dogs, houses
ch	chin, such, match		zh	vision, treasure, seizure

DICTIONARY

A

ac•cu•rate (ak´yər it) *adj.* Without errors; exact and correct. page 114

a•chieve•ment (ə chēv´mənt) *n.* Something that has been done through great effort. Learning to play the violin is a great achievement. page 66

a•dult•hood (ə dult´hùd´) *n.* The state of being fully grown-up. page 78

ad•van•tage (ad van´tij) *n.* A better position from which to get something; an edge. Being tall is an advantage for a basketball player. page 66

aer•i•al (âr´ē əl) *adj.* Of or in the air. page 47

aide (ād) *n.* Helper. page 114

air•borne (âr´bôrn´) *adj.* Off the ground; carried by the air. page 30

al•ien (āl´yən, ā´lē ən) *adj.* From another planet. page 119

a•loft (ə lôft´) *adv.* Up in the air. page 30

al•ter•nate (ôl´tər nit) *n.* A person who can act in the place of another; substitute. page 61

al•ti•tude (al´ti tüd´, al´ti tūd´) *n.* Height; the distance above the ground. page 30

am•bi•tious (am bish´əs) *adj.* Having a strong desire to do something; wishing for something better. page 119

ar•chae•ol•o•gist (är´kē ol´ə jist) *n.* A scientist who studies people who lived long ago. page 6

ar•ti•fact (är´tə fakt´) *n.* Something made by people long ago. Buttons, knives, and other artifacts were found under the old house. page 6

ar•ti•fi•cial (är´tə fish´əl) *adj.* Not real or natural; built by people. page 102

as•sign•ment (ə sīn´mənt) *n.* Job; the work someone is given to do. page 47

as•sist•ance (ə sis´təns) *n.* Help. page 102

ath•let•ic (ath let´ik) *adj.* Having to do with sports. page 54

at•ten•tive (ə ten´tiv) *adj.* Looking closely; paying careful attention. page 90

at•tract (ə trakt´) *v.* To get the attention of; draw to oneself. Flowers and sweet smells attract bees. page 90

at•trac•tive (ə trak´tiv) *adj.* Pleasing; getting others' attention and approval. page 71

au•thor•i•ty (ə thôr´i tē) *n.* The power to give orders. page 78

au•to•mat•ic (ô´tə mat´ik) *adj.* Able to operate by itself. page 102

a•vi•a•tion (ā´vē ā´shən, av´ē ā´shən) *n.* Flying in balloons or airplanes. page 30

B

bar•na•cle (bär´nə kəl) *n.* A small, shelled sea animal that clings to rocks and ships' bottoms. page 13

bar•ri•er (bar´ē ər) *n.* A wall; something that is in the way. page 54

be•hav•ior (bi hāv´yər) *n.* Way of acting. Eating cake for breakfast is unhealthy behavior. page-90

bil•low (bil´ō) *n.* A large wave. page 23

black•smith (blak´smith´) *n.* A person who makes things out of iron, using a furnace and hammer. page 12

brace•let (brās´lit) *n.* Jewelry worn around the arm or wrist. page 18

bu•oy (bü´ē, boi) *n.* A float used as a warning or marker. page 23

bus•tle (bus´əl) *v.* bus•tled, bus•tling To hurry in a noisy way. The cook in his stiff uniform bustled about the kitchen. page 78

C _____

cap•sule (kap´səl) *n.* The part of a spaceship that carries people. page 47

cap•tive (kap´tiv) *adj.* Kept in a prison. page 36

car•a•van (kar´ə van´) *n.* A group of people traveling together for safety, especially in the desert. page 84

cham•ber (chām´bər) *n.* A room. page 6

cir•cu•lar (sûr´kyə lər) *adj.* Round like a dinner plate. page 95

civ•i•li•za•tion (siv´ə lə zā´shən) *n.* The society and culture of a people. page 6

clash (klash) *v.* To fight; have a conflict. page 119

clip•board (klip´bôrd´) *n.* A board for writing that has a clip to hold papers in place. page 108

cob•web (kob´web´) *n.* A dusty, tangled spider's web. page 95

cock•pit (kok´pit´) *n.* The place where a pilot sits; the control center of a space shuttle. page 47

com•mand•er (kə man´dər) *n.* The person who gives orders; the person in charge. page 47

con•ceal (kən sēl´) *v.* To hide. page 90

con•nec•tion (kə nek´shən) *n.* The place where two parts are joined. The connection between the old wire and the lamp was broken. page 108

con•sid•er•a•ble (kən sid´ər ə bəl) *adj.* Much. page 71

con•vey•or belt (kən vā´ər belt) *n.* A wide, moving belt used in factories to move parts from place to place. page 108

co•op•er•ate (kō op´ə rāt´) *v.* co•op•er•at•ed, co•op•er•at•ing To work together. The class cooperated on painting a school mural. page 78

cou•ra•geous (kə rā´jəs) *adj.* Very brave. page 54

cred•it (kred´it) *n.* Recognition that a student has completed a course of study. page 61

crev•ice (krev´is) *n.* Crack; narrow split. page 13

D _____

de•bris (də brē´, dā´brē) *n.* Rubbish; scattered bits and pieces. page 13

ded•i•cat•ed (ded´i kā´tid) *adj.* Willing to work with great loyalty; devoted. The dedicated nurse sat all night by the sick child's bed. page 47

de•fend (di fend´) *v.* To keep safe; guard. page 78

de•pen•da•ble (di pen´də bəl) *adj.* Able to be trusted. page 119

de•scent (di sent´) *n.* Downward movement. page-13

des•ti•na•tion (des´tə nā´shən) *n.* The place to which someone is going. page 23

de•vice (di vīs´) *n.* Something made and used by people; a machine. page 102

de•vote (di vōt´) *v.* de•vo•ted, de•vot•ing To give up time to an activity. The skater devoted many hours to perfecting her spin. page 30

de•vour (di vour´) *v.* To eat. page 90

di•am•e•ter (dī am´i tər) *n.* The distance across a circle. page 95

di•gest (di jest´, dī jest´) *v.* To change food in the stomach to forms the body can use. page 90

dis•ci•pline (dis´ə plin) *n.* Training and self-control. page 71

dis•cov•er•er (dis kuv´ər ər) *n.* A person who finds something. page 23

dis•tin•guish (di sting´gwish) *v.* To see the differences. Can you distinguish between the footprints of a rabbit and a coyote? page 42

draft (draft) *n.* A drink. page 37

drift•wood (drift´wŭd´) *n.* Wood that has washed ashore. page 12

dwell (dwel) *v.* dwelt or dwelled, dwell•ing To live in a place. page 85

E

ef•fi•cient (i fish´ənt) *adj.* Working without wasting time or energy. page 114

e•lab•o•rate (i lab´ər it) *adj.* Complicated; having many parts. The teacher's elaborate directions made the game of bridge seem impossible to learn. page 119

em•er•ald (em´ər əld) *n.* A gem that is deep green in color. page 18

em•ploy•ee (em ploi´ē, em´ploi ē´) *n.* A person who works for someone else. page 114

en•a•ble (e nā´bəl, i nā´bəl) *v.* en•a•bled, en•a•bling To allow; give the ability. page 30

en•cir•cle (en sûr´kəl) *v.* en•cir•cled, en•cir•cling To go around; surround. page 95

e•qual•i•ty (i kwol´i tē) *n.* The state of being equal, in which everyone is treated the same way. page 54

e•quip (i kwip´) *v.* e•quipped, e•quip•ping To furnish; supply. page 102

e•ra (îr´ə, er´ə) *n.* A period of history. The good feelings between the U.S. and the U.S.S.R. cooled in the postwar era. page 114

es•sen•tial (i sen´shəl) *adj.* Very important; necessary. page 71

ev•i•dence (ev´i dəns) *n.* A sign that something is there or has happened. A handshake is evidence of good will. page 23

ev•i•dent (ev´i dənt) *adj.* Easy to see or tell; plain. page 6

ex•hi•bi•tion (ek´sə bish´ən) *n.* A public display of objects or skills. page 71

ex•ist•ence (eg zis´təns) *n.* Being. page 78

ex•pand (ek spand´) *v.* To become larger. page 30

ex•pe•di•tion (ek´spi dish´ən) *n.* A journey with a special purpose. page 6

eye•sight (ī´sīt´) *n.* The power of seeing. page 42

F

fab•u•lous (fab´yə ləs) *adj.* Imaginary; as if out of a fable. page 30

Fahr•en•heit (far´ən hīt´) *adj.* Relating to a temperature scale where water freezes at 32 degrees and boils at 212 degrees. page 18

fas•ci•na•tion (fas´ə nā´shən) *n.* A strong attraction to something. Today's young people feel a fascination for computers. page 119

fear•some (fîr´səm) *adj.* Scary; frightening. page-42

feat (fēt) *n.* A great or unusual act. The feat performed by Atlas was to hold the world on his shoulders. page 30

field•er (fēl´dər) *n.* A baseball player who tries to catch and throw balls hit to the field. page 54

flex•i•ble (flek´sə bəl) *adj.* Able to bend and not break. page 95

frag•ile (fraj´əl) *adj.* Not strong; weak. page 95

G

gal•ax•y (gal´ək sē) *n.* gal•ax•ies A large group of stars. page 119

gal•le•on (gal´ē ən) *n.* A large sailing ship used in the 1400s and 1500s. page 12

gem (jem) *n.* A stone that is worth a lot of money; a stone used in jewelry. page 18

gi•gan•tic (jī gan´tik) *adj.* Very large; huge. page-109

glim•mer (glim´ər) *v.* To appear to give off a dim light. page 18

grav•i•ta•tion•al (grav´i tā´shən əl) *adj.* Having to do with gravity, or the force that pulls things toward the center of the earth. The gravitational pull of the earth makes an apple fall down instead of up. page 47

grit (grit) *n.* Small pieces of sand or stone. page 84

H

hab•i•tat (hab´i tat´) *n.* The sort of place where a certain animal usually lives. The ability to go without water suits a camel to its desert habitat. page 42

hand•hold (hand´hōld´) *n.* Something to take hold of with the hands. page 13

ha•ven (hā´vən) *n.* A shelter; a safe place. The island was a haven for seagulls and their young. page 84

hi•ber•nate (hī´bər nāt´) *v.* hi•ber•nat•ed, hi•ber•nat•ing To spend the winter sleeping. page 42

his•tor•ic (hi stôr´ik) *adj.* Very important; likely to be remembered for a long time. page 6

hor•i•zon•tal (hôr´ə zon´təl, hor´ə zon´təl) *adj.* Flat; going across. page 95

hull (hul) *n.* The frame of a ship. page 23

I

im•pris•oned (im priz´ənd) *adj.* Locked up; put in prison. page 36

im•prove•ment (im prüv´mənt) *n.* A change for the better. page 66

in•di•cate (in´di kāt´) *v.* in•di•cat•ed, in•di•cat•ing To show; point out. The compass needle indicated the boat was off course. page-66

in•flu•ence (in´flü əns) *n.* Power over others. The influence of his father made the boy choose swimming as his sport. page 54

in•jured (in´jərd) *adj.* Hurt; damaged. page 61

in•struct (in strukt´) *v.* To show how; teach. page-47

in•struc•tor (in struk´tər) *n.* A teacher. page 66

in•tel•li•gence (in tel´i jəns) *n.* Mind; the ability to learn and think. page 102

in•ves•ti•gate (in ves´ti gāt´) *v.* in•ves•ti•gat•ed, in•ves•ti•gat•ing To look into with great care. page 6

J

jew•el•ry (jü´əl rē) *n.* Decorations for the body; rings, bracelets, and necklaces. page 18

A

key•board (kē´bôrd´) *n.* A set of keys with letters on them used to put information into a computer. page 109

L

land•mark (land´märk´) *n.* Something easily seen, used to determine one's location. page 84

lift•off (lift´ôf´) *n.* The act of rising from the ground and taking flight. page 47

long-term (lông´tûrm´) *adj.* Involving a number of years. They had a long-term relationship. page 60

M

ma•chin•er•y (mə shē´nə rē) *n.* Machines; objects with parts that move and do work. page 114

main•mast (mān´mast´, mān´məst) *n.* The pole on a ship that holds the largest sail. page 12

main•tain (mān tān´) *v.* To keep in a certain state. page 71

ma•neu•ver (mə nü´vər) *v.* To keep in a certain state. page 114

man•tle (man´təl) *n.* The layer of the earth that is just under the top layer, or crust. page 18

man•u•fac•tur•er (man´yə fak´chər ər) *n.* The owner of a factory. page 114

mer•chan•dise (mûr´chən dīz´, mûr´chən dīs´) *n.* Goods sold in stores. page 102

mesh (mesh) *n.* A net of connected threads. page-85

mi•gra•tion (mī grā´shən) *n.* Movement from one place to another. The migration of the monarch butterfly covers thousands of miles. page 42

mor•tal (môr´təl) *n.* A human being. A romance between the god Zeus and a mortal can cause trouble. page 36

N

nav•i•gate (nav´i gāt´) *v.* nav•i•gat•ed, nav•i•gat•ing To steer a boat or plane. page 23

O

ob•sta•cle (ob´stə kəl) *n.* Something that is in the way. Romeo overcame all obstacles to win Juliet's love. page 42

or•gan•i•za•tion (ôr´gə nə zā´shən) *n.* An arrangement of parts to make a whole. page 78

out•stand•ing (out´stan´ding) *adj.* Better than others; standing out from the rest. page 71

o•ver•took (ō´vər tůk´) *v.* past tense of overtake; o•ver•tak•en, o•ver•tak•ing Caught up with. page 37

P

pan•el (pan´əl) *n.* A group of people chosen for a specific purpose. page 61

par•a•lyze (par´ə līz´) *v.* par•a•lyzed, par•a•lyz•ing To make something unable to move. page 90

per•son•al•i•ty (pûr´sə nal´i tē) *n.* per•son•al•i•ties The group of qualities that make one person different from another. page 109

poi•son•ous (poi´zə nəs) *adj.* Containing a substance that can cause sickness or death. page-90

pop•u•lar•i•ty (pop´yə lar´i tē) *n.* Being liked by many people. page 54

pos•i•tive (poz´i tiv) *adj.* Confident and sure; not doubting. page 66

pre•cise (pri sīs´) *adj.* Very careful and exact. Precise measurements make eye surgery possible. page 71

prej•u•dice (prej´ə dis) *n.* Unfair dislike of a group of people. page 54

prep•a•ra•tion (prep´ə rā´shən) *n.* Something done to get ready. page 66

prey (prā) *v.* To hunt and kill. The eagle preys on deer and small animals. page 42

print•out (print´out´) *n.* The printed results of work by a computer. page 109

pro•ce•dure (prə sē´jər) *n.* Steps taken to reach a goal. The procedure for making an origami bird is hard to learn. page 66

pro•duc•tion (prə duk´shən) *n.* The process of making something; the act of creating. page 108

pro•vince (prov´ins) *n.* provinces A large region of a country. page 60

pur•suit (pər süt´) *n.* The act of chasing something. The posse has been in pursuit of the bandit for two days. page 84

pyr•a•mid (pir´ə mid´) *n.* A huge pointed building made of stone. page 6

Q

quiz (kwiz) *v.* quizzed, quiz•zing To question closely. page 60

R

re•build (rē bild´) *v.* re•built To make again; build again. page 102

rec•og•ni•tion (rek´əg nish´ən) *n.* Fame; attention given someone who has done something good. page 54

rec•om•mend (rek´ə mend´) *v.* To speak in favor of. page 30

rec•tan•gle (rek´tang´gəl) *n.* A four-sided shape with four right angles and two sides that are longer than the other two. page 95

reel (rēl) *v.* To whirl; feel dizzy. page 37

re•search (ri sûrch´, rē´sûrch´) *n.* A study to find out facts. page 66

rig•or•ous (rig´ər əs) *adj.* Strict and difficult. The rigorous training required him to run twenty miles each day. page 71

ro•bot (rō´bət, rō´bot) *n.* A machine that copies the actions of people. page 102

ro•dent (rō´dənt) *n.* A type of mammal that gnaws with its teeth, such as a mouse. page 42

ro•tate (rō´tāt) *v.* ro•tat•ed, ro•tat•ing To turn. page 102

rou•tine (rü tēn´) *n.* A set of movements done over and over in the same way. The athlete's routine includes starting each day with a good breakfast. page 60

ru•by (rü´bē) *n.* ru•bies A gem that is deep red in color. page 18

S

sap•phire (saf´īr) *n.* A gem that is blue in color. page 18

scu•ba (skü´bə) *adj.* Using equipment for breathing underwater. page 23

scut•tle (skut´əl) *v.* scut•tled, scut•tling To move with quick, short steps. The black beetle scuttled across the kitchen floor. page 84

sen•ior (sēn´yər) *adj.* Higher in rank; advanced; older. page 61

sen•sa•tion (sen sā´shən) *n.* Feeling. page 47

se•quence (sē´kwəns) *n.* An arrangement in which one thing follows another in a particular order. page 71

sift (sift) *v.* To fall; be sprinkled. The snow sifted down the chimney onto the hearth. page 84

sil•hou•ette (sil´ü et´) *v.* sil•hou•et•ted, sil•hou•et•ting To form a dark outline against a light background. page 85

smock (smok) *n.* A long, loose shirt worn to protect clothes. page 108

so•lar (sō´lər) *adj.* Operated by the sun's energy. page 108

spe•cial•ize (spesh´ə līz´) *v.* spe•cial•ized, spe•cial•iz•ing To have a particular way of acting. page 90

spe•cies (spē´shēz) *n.* A group of plants or animals that have certain common features. Warblers belong to a large species of songbirds. page 42

spin•y (spī´nē) *adj.* spin•i•er, spin•i•est Having pointed spines or thorns. page 12

strength•en (strengk´thən, streng´thən, stren´thən) *v.* To make stronger. page 66

sunk•en (sung´kən) *adj.* Resting under the water. page 23

superb (sü pûrb´) *adj.* Very good; excellent. page-54

sus•pend (sə spend´) *v.* To hang from something fastened above. page 95

sus•tained (sə stānd´) *adj.* Supported; held up. The climbers were sustained by spikes and ropes. page 37

T

tech•ni•cian (tek nish´ən) *n.* A person who is skilled at using machinery. page 114

teem•ing (tēm´ing) *adj.* Full; crowded. It was easy to get lost in the teeming streets of Hong Kong. page 78

threat (thret) *n.* A sign of danger. The black clouds were a threat to our picnic. page 78

tire•less (tīr´lis) *adj.* Never becoming tired; never stopping. page 78

tomb (tüm) *n.* A grave; a place for a dead body. page 6

tu•tor (tü´tər, tu´tər) *n.* A private instructor. page-60

U

un•der•sea (un´dər sē´, un´dər sē´) *adj.* Beneath the surface of the sea. page 23

un•earth (un ûrth´) *v.* To dig out of the ground. page 18

up•lift•ed (up lif´tid) *adj.* Raised up and held in the air. page 37

V

vague•ly (vāg´lē) *adv.* In an unclear way; dimly. page 37

va•ri•e•ty (və rī´i tē) *n.* va•ri•e•ties A number of different kinds. page 114

veer (vîr) *v.* To change direction. page 36

ver•sion (vûr´zhən) *n.* A special form. page 119

ver•ti•cal (vûr´ti kəl) *adj.* In an up-and-down direction. page 95

vic•tim (vik´təm) *n.* A person or animal which is harmed or killed by another. The injured dog was a victim of a careless driver. page 90

view•er (vū´ər) *n.* A person who looks at or watches something. page 119

vil•lain (vil´ən) *n.* A wicked person. page 119

Answer Key

UNIT 1
Buried Treasure

LESSON 1
Egyptian Tomb Discovered

Context Clues

1. archaeologists
2. civilization
3. expedition
4. pyramids
5. tombs
6. chambers
7. investigate
8. historic
9. artifacts
10. evident

Word Groups

1. tomb
2. archaeologist
3. expedition

Cloze Paragraph

1. tomb
2. investigated
3. historic
4. civilization
5. artifacts
6. Archaeologists
7. evident
8. expedition

Crossword Puzzle

Across
1. investigate
4. archaeologists
5. pyramids
6. tombs
7. chambers
8. civilization
9. historic

Down
2. evident
3. expedition
4. artifacts

Get Wise to Tests

1. search into
2. graves
3. room
4. trip
5. easy to see
6. scientists
7. important
8. group of people
9. huge buildings
10. objects

Writing

Answers will vary based on students' personal experiences.

LESSON 2
Treasure at Blue Beach

Using Context

1. driftwood
2. blacksmith
3. spiny
4. descent
5. galleon
6. handhold
7. mainmast
8. barnacles
9. debris
10. crevice

Challenge Yourself

Possible responses: cliffs, brick or stone wall; horseshoes, tools for fireplaces

Compound Words

1. driftwood
2. mainmast
3. handhold
4. blacksmith

Word Origins

1. spiny
2. galleon
3. crevice
4. descent
5. debris
6. barnacles

Get Wise to Tests

1. D   3. C   5. A   7. D   9. D
2. F   4. F   6. G   8. G   10. F

Review

1. A   2. H   3. D   4. G

Writing

Answers will vary.

LESSON 3
Gems

Context Clues

1. Gems
2. glimmer
3. Fahrenheit
4. mantle
5. unearth
6. jewelry
7. Emeralds
8. ruby
9. sapphire
10. bracelets

Challenge Yourself

Possible responses: jewels, sparkles

Analogies

1. sapphire
2. bracelet
3. jewelry
4. ruby

Dictionary Skills

1. emerald, Fahrenheit, gems, glimmer;
2. jewelry, mantle, sapphire, unearth

Get Wise to Tests

1. C   3. C   5. C   7. C   9. B
2. F   4. F   6. F   8. H   10. H

Review

1. D   2. H   3. A   4. G   5. D

Writing

Answers will vary.

LESSON 4
Treasures From the Deep

Context Clues

1. sunken
2. destination
3. navigate
4. hull
5. evidence
6. discoverers
7. buoy
8. undersea
9. billows
10. scuba

Word Origins

1. navigate
2. hull
3. evidence
4. scuba

Cloze Paragraph

1. undersea
2. sunken
3. billows
4. buoy
5. destination
6. discoverers

World Map

Who Finds Treasure: discoverers
Where Treasure Is Found: sunken, undersea
Things Used to Hunt Treasure: scuba, buoy
Kinds of Treasure Found: possible responses: gold coins, jewels

Get Wise to Tests

1. B   3. C   5. B   7. C   9. D
2. F   4. I   6. G   8. F   10. G

Review

1. A   2. G

Writing

Answers will vary.

UNIT 2
Up, Up, and Away

LESSON 5
Ballooning

Context Clues

1. devote
2. recommend
3. aviation
4. fabulous
5. feat
6. expanded
7. enables
8. altitude
9. aloft
10. airborne

Writing Sentences

Answers will vary.

Cloze Paragraph

1. aviation
2. devote
3. recommend
4. enables

Tangled-Up Words

1. aviation
2. recommend
3. enables
4. altitude
5. feat
6. expanded
7. aloft
8. fabulous
9. airborne
10. devote

Get Wise to Tests

1. C   3. A   5. A   7. C   9. A
2. I   4. G   6. I   8. G   10. G

Review

1. B   2. F   3. C   4. F   5. C

Writing

Answers will vary.

LESSON 6
Icarus and Daedalus

Using Context

1. mortals
2. reel
3. captive
4. overtook
5. draft
6. vaguely
7. uplifted
8. veered
9. imprisoned
10. sustained

Challenge Yourself

Possible responses: people, animals; jail, castle

Synonyms

1. prisoner
2. supported
3. drink
4. whirl
5. shift
6. raised

Antonyms

1. vaguely
2. overlook
3. uplifted
4. imprisoned
5. mortals
6. captive

Get Wise to Tests

1. D 3. B 5. A 7. C 9. B
2. F 4. I 6. H 8. I 10. F

Review

1. C 2. G

Writing

Answers will vary.

LESSON 7
Night Flights

Using Context

1. rodent   6. eyesight
2. distinguish   7. hibernate
3. species   8. obstacle
4. fearsome   9. migration
5. prey   10. habitat

Challenge Yourself

Possible responses: squirrel, bird;
monster, lion

Dictionary Skills

1. migration   5. distinguish
2. species   6. prey
3. eyesight   7. habitat
4. hibernate   8. fearsome

Classifying

1. obstacles   4. fearsome
2. rodents   5. habitats
3. species   6. prey

Get Wise to Tests

1. C 3. A 5. C 7. B 9. D
2. G 4. F 6. I 8. F 10. F

Review

1. A 2. G

Writing

Answers will vary based on students'
personal experiences.

LESSON 8
Walking in Space

Context Clues

1. dedicated   5. commander
2. instructed   6. gravitational
3. assignment,   7. sensation
   capsule   8. cockpit
4. liftoff   9. aerial

Challenge Yourself

Possible responses: oceans, continents;
stock shelves, deliver a package

Synonyms

1. devoted   4. taught
2. feeling   5. job
3. chief   6. skyward

Word Sense

1. no   6. yes
2. yes   7. no
3. yes   8. yes
4. no   9. no
5. no

Crossword Puzzle

Across   Down
4. gravitational   1. liftoff
7. dedicated   2. instructed
8. commander   3. sensation
9. capsule   5. assignment
10. cockpit   6. aerial

Get Wise to Tests

1. C 3. A 5. A 7. D 9. B
2. F 4. H 6. G 8. F 10. F

Writing

Answers will vary based on students'
personal experiences.

UNIT 3
Sports Watch

LESSON 9
Marvelous Jackie Robinson

Using Context

1. influence   6. fielder
2. barrier   7. popularity
3. equality   8. athletic
4. courageous   9. recognition
5. superb   10. prejudice

Challenge Yourself

Possible responses: a relative, a friend

Related Words

1. athletic   4. courageous
2. recognition   5. equality
3. popularity   6. superb

Writing Sentences

Answers will vary.

Tangled-Up Words

1. athletic   6. courageous
2. fielder   7. influence
3. popularity   8. superb
4. barrier   9. prejudice
5. equality   10. recognition

Get Wise to Tests

1. A 3. D 5. C 7. D 9. B
2. G 4. I 6. F 8. G 10. F

Review

1. B 2. F

Writing

Answers will vary based on students'
personal experiences.

LESSON 10
Full Speed Ahead

Using Context

1. injured   6. senior
2. alternate   7. credit
3. quiz   8. provinces
4. routine   9. tutor
5. long-term   10. panel

Challenge Yourself

Possible responses: becoming a teacher,
becoming a nurse; dancing, gymnastics

Multiple Meanings

1. b 2. a 3. b 4. a

Analogies

1. senior   6. tutor
2. long-term   7. credit
3. quiz   8. alternate
4. injured   9. panel
5. provinces

Get Wise to Tests

1. C 3. C 5. B 7. C 9. C
2. I 4. H 6. I 8. I 10. F

Review

1. B 2. F

Writing

Answers will vary based on students'
personal experiences.

LESSON 11
Mind and Body

Using Context

1. advantage   6. strengthen
2. instructor   7. indicates
3. positive   8. research
4. procedure   9. improvement
5. achievement   10. preparation

Challenge Yourself

Possible responses: cooking, taking a
test; running a race, performing in a play

Word Groups

1. improvement   4. achievement
2. procedure   5. preparation
3. instructor

Cloze Paragraph

1. indicates   4. strengthen
2. research   5. advantage
3. positive

Get Wise to Tests

1. a help   6. teacher
2. method   7. study
3. progress   8. make stronger
4. success   9. confident
   at a goal   10. training
5. shows

Review

1. leader   4. brave
2. excellent   5. unfairness
3. kinds

Writing

Answers will vary based on students'
personal experiences.

LESSON 12
She's Really on the Ball!

Using Context
1. rigorous
2. essential
3. precise
4. discipline
5. maintain
6. considerable
7. exhibition
8. outstanding
9. sequence
10. attractive

Challenge Yourself
Possible responses: food, water; get ready for school, go to classes at school

Word Groups
1. considerable
2. maintain
3. attractive
4. exhibition
5. essential
6. rigorous
7. outstanding
8. discipline
9. sequence
10. precise

Word Origins
1. sequence
2. rigorous
3. discipline

Word Sense
Possible responses:
1. yes
2. attractive person
3. yes
4. yes
5. popular exhibition
6. rigorous training
7. yes

Writing Sentences
Answers will vary.

Get Wise to Tests
1. C
2. F
3. D
4. H
5. B
6. F
7. A
8. H
9. B
10. I

Review
1. B
2. F
3. D
4. F

Writing
Answers will vary based on students' personal experiences.

UNIT 4
Small Worlds

LESSON 13
A Well-Ordered World

Using Context
1. organization
2. adulthood
3. bustle
4. teeming
5. tireless
6. cooperate
7. existence
8. authority
9. threat
10. defend

Challenge Yourself
Possible responses: Girl Scouts/Boy Scouts, 4-H Club; teacher, police officer

Writing Sentences
Answers will vary.

Cloze Paragraph
1. defend
2. threat
3. cooperate
4. teeming
5. bustle
6. authority

Word Maps
Jobs of Worker Ants: defend
Ways Ants Act: cooperate, bustle, tireless
About the Ant Colony Queen: organization, authority

Get Wise to Tests
1. C
2. G
3. B
4. I
5. A
6. H
7. C
8. F
9. B
10. I

Review
1. D
2. G
3. A
4. F

Writing
Answers will vary.

LESSON 14
The Prophet and the Spider

Context Clues
1. caravan
2. landmark
3. silhouetted
4. grit
5. sifted
6. pursuit
7. haven
8. dwelling
9. scuttled
10. mesh

Multiple Meanings
1. a
2. b
3. b
4. a

Cloze Paragraph
1. caravan
2. pursuit
3. mesh
4. silhouetted
5. sifted
6. scuttled
7. dwelling
8. haven

Get Wise to Tests
1. C
2. G
3. A
4. I
5. B
6. F
7. D
8. G
9. C
10. H

Review
1. A
2. H

Writing
Answers will vary based on students' personal experiences.

LESSON 15
Insect Self Defense

Using Context
1. behavior
2. specialize
3. victims
4. devour
5. conceal
6. attract
7. poisonous
8. digest
9. paralyzed
10. attentive

Challenge Yourself
Possible responses: snakes, mushrooms; peanut butter, popcorn

Word Groups
1. poisonous
2. devour
3. conceal
4. behavior
5. attentive
6. paralyzed
7. attract

Word Sense
Possible responses:
1. digest food
2. unhappy victims
3. yes
4. yes
5. paralyzed animal
6. attentive guard
7. yes

Get Wise to Tests
1. D
2. G
3. C
4. F
5. A
6. I
7. A
8. H
9. B
10. I

Writing
Answers will vary based on students' personal experiences.

LESSON 16
Spiders Are Builders

Using Context
1. horizontal
2. encircle
3. cobwebs
4. fragile
5. diameter
6. suspends
7. vertical
8. circular
9. rectangles
10. flexible

Challenge Yourself
Possible responses: glass, baby; balloon, light fixture

Analogies
1. fragile
2. cobwebs
3. rectangles
4. flexible
5. circular
6. suspends

Writing Sentences
Answers will vary.

Hidden Message Puzzle
1. encircle
2. vertical
3. flexible
4. rectangles
5. cobwebs
6. horizontal
7. suspends
8. fragile
Answer to puzzle: catching flies!

Get Wise to Tests
1. B
2. F
3. C
4. I
5. B
6. F
7. B
8. F
9. D
10. F

Review
1. A
2. I
3. C
4. G
5. C

Writing
Answers will vary.

UNIT 5
Remarkable Robots

LESSON 17
How Robots Came to Be

Context Clues

1. robots
2. automatic
3. assistance
4. device
5. artificial
6. equipped
7. rotate
8. rebuilt
9. intelligence
10. merchandise

Classifying

Names for These Machines: robots, device, merchandise
Qualities of These Machines: artificial, automatic

Dictionary Skills

Possible responses:
1. It is full of equipment.
2. It spins.
3. It is not built again.
4. yes
5. You are giving them help.
6. yes

Crossword Puzzle

Across
1. assistance
5. robots
7. device
8. merchandise

Down
1. artificial
2. intelligence
3. automatic
4. equipped
5. rebuilt
6. rotate

Get Wise to Tests

1. C 3. A 5. A 7. B 9. C
2. G 4. I 6. H 8. I 10. F

Writing

Answers will vary.

LESSON 18
My Robot Buddy

Context Clues

1. solar
2. gigantic
3. smock
4. clipboard
5. conveyor belt
6. production
7. connections
8. keyboards
9. printout
10. personality

Word Groups

1. clipboard
2. smock
3. keyboard
4. connections
5. gigantic
6. conveyor belt

Dictionary Skills

1. solar; a
2. production; a
3. personality; b
4. printout; b

Get Wise to Tests

1. B 3. A 5. B 7. C 9. D
2. F 4. H 6. I 8. F 10. H

Review

1. C 2. I

Writing

Answers will vary.

LESSON 19
What a Worker!

Context Clues

1. machinery
2. technician
3. variety
4. aide
5. manufacturer
6. employee
7. era
8. maneuver
9. efficient
10. accurate

Word Sense

Possible responses:
1. robot manufacturer
2. yes
3. heavy machinery
4. accurate directions
5. parent's aide

Cloze Paragraph

1. era
2. employee
3. technicians
4. maneuver
5. efficient
6. variety

Get Wise to Tests

1. C 3. A 5. C 7. B 9. A
2. G 4. G 6. F 8. G 10. G

Review

1. B 2. F 3. C 4. I 5. A

Writing

Answers will vary based on students' personal experiences.

LESSON 20
Real Art?

Using Context

1. viewers
2. version
3. dependable
4. clashed
5. alien
6. fascination
7. villains
8. ambitious
9. elaborate
10. galaxies

Challenge Yourself

Possible responses: at a movie, at a baseball game; Catwoman, Dracula

Antonyms

1. elaborate
2. fascination
3. dependable
4. ambitious
5. alien

Rewriting Sentences

1. I have always wanted to visit other galaxies.
2. I would take along my dependable robot.
3. We would fight and conquer many villains.
4. I could write a book, and it could be made into a movie version.

Related Words

1. fascination
2. viewers
3. elaborate
4. dependable
5. ambitious

Word Sense

Possible responses:
1. yes
2. dishonest villains
3. ambitious workers
4. yes
5. alien creature
6. yes
7. dependable neighbors

Get Wise to Tests

1. B 3. B 5. A 7. A 9. C
2. I 4. F 6. H 8. I 10. G

Review

1. C 2. F

Writing

Answers will vary.

UNIT 1 Review

1. pyramids
2. jewelry
3. spiny
4. investigate
5. buoy
6. historic
7. navigate
8. glimmer
9. sunken
10. debris

UNIT 2 Review

1. yes
2. no
3. no
4. no
5. yes
6. yes
7. yes
8. no
9. no
10. yes
11. no
12. yes

UNIT 3 Review

1. maintain
2. prejudice
3. superb
4. sequence
5. strengthen
6. injured
7. positive
8. long-term
9. alternate
10. popularity

UNIT 4 Review

1. fragile
2. conceal
3. haven
4. vertical
5. grit
6. authority
7. suspends
8. attentive
9. defend
10. caravan

UNIT 5 Review

1. no
2. yes
3. yes
4. no
5. yes
6. no
7. yes
8. yes
9. no
10. no
11. no
12. yes

REVIEW AND WRITE

Answers will vary based on students' personal experiences.